Understanding & Using Spoken Language

Understanding & Using Spoken Language

Games for 7 to 9 Year Olds

Catherine Delamain & Jill Spring

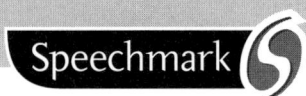

Speechmark (S)

Speechmark Publishing
Telford Road, Bicester, Oxon OX26 4LQ, UK

Please note that in this text, for reasons of clarity alone,
'he' is used to refer to the child and 'she' to the teacher.

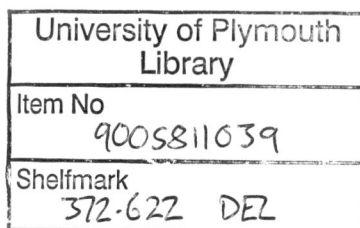

First published in 2004 by
Speechmark Publishing Ltd, Telford Road, Bicester, Oxon OX26 4LQ, UK

www.speechmark.net

© Catherine Delamain & Jill Spring, 2004

002-5183/Printed in the United Kingdom/1010

British Library Cataloguing in Publication Data
Delamain, Catherine
      Understanding & using spoken language: games for 7 to 9 year olds
      1. Communicative competence in children – Study and teaching (Elementary) – Great Britain
      2. English language – Spoken language – Study and teaching (Elementary) – Great Britain
      3. Listening   4. Educational games
      I. Title   II. Spring, Jill
      372.6′044′0941

ISBN 0 86388 515 2

Contents

1 UNDERSTANDING SPOKEN LANGUAGE

2 USING SPOKEN LANGUAGE

3 ACTIVITY RESOURCES

Contents

Preface

'Language has a unique role in capturing the breadth of human thought and endeavour'

(D Crystal, *Cambridge Encyclopaedia of Language*)

This book provides a sequel to *Games for Speaking, Listening & Understanding* (Delamain & Spring, 2003). It contains a collection of activities designed to foster the language skills of children in Key Stage II of the National Curriculum of England and Wales, in Years 3 and 4. These children will range in age from seven to nine years.

The book aims to provide teachers with practical strategies for the development of speaking and understanding. The authors are both experienced speech and language therapists who have worked extensively alongside mainstream teachers for many years. As pioneers in the development of collaborative practice between the two professions they are keenly aware of the benefits of shared expertise.

Every effort has been made to minimise paperwork, and to make the activities both teacher- and child- friendly.

Understanding & Using Spoken Language: Games for Seven- to Nine-Year-Olds offers:

◆ A wide range of carefully structured activities

◆ Clear aims and instructions

◆ An extensive resource section

◆ Opportunities for assessment, target-setting and evaluation

Acknowledgements

The authors would like to thank the staff in all the schools in which they have tried out these activities. Particular thanks go to Gillingham Primary School, Damers First School, and Winterbourne Valley First School, all of which are in Dorset. Thanks also to Mrs Men Bao for permission to adapt some *qi gung* exercises for use as warm-up activities.

'Poetry Please' drew on several sources for the poems, some of which had to be slightly altered to avoid naming the object being described. Thanks are due to Percy H. Ilott, Rose Fyleman, Eileen Mathias, E.E. Gould, Mary E. Coleridge, and John R. Crossland. Thanks and apologies are due to Pam Ayres, whose poems *In Defence of Hedgehogs* and *The Bunny Poem* were altered or added to.

Introduction

'Language comes so naturally to us that it is easy to forget what a strange and miraculous gift it is.'

(Stephen Pinker, *Words and Rules*)

Language is a key component in most areas of human intelligence, and is fundamental to learning. In the school context, language competence becomes increasingly important as the demands of the curriculum increase.

In recent years the importance of speaking and listening skills has been increasingly recognised, and this is reflected in National Curriculum targets. The DfES has published a national strategy for the development of Speaking, Listening and Learning in Key Stages 1 and 2. (Qualifications and Curriculum Authority, November 2003.) This document emphasises the importance of making time for the development of oral language skills across the curriculum, and is therefore most welcome.

The guidance offers teaching objectives and classroom activities.

However, these assume a considerable degree of pre-existing language competence. Many children will need to practise some of the specific underlying skills before they are ready to take full advantage of these new opportunities.

Understanding & Using Spoken Language provides a range of activities that can be considered as the building blocks on which effective communication is founded.

Research has shown that in a mainstream classroom children are allowed very little time to express their thoughts, ideas and feelings orally. Debate, argument and discussion tend to be teacher-led, and restricted in the interests of class control and conflict avoidance. The games in this book give legitimate outlets for self-expression within a structured context. They offer opportunities for developing the skills of attentive listening, thinking, reasoning, describing, debating and speaking with clarity.

These games are designed to foster the speaking and listening skills described in the Key Stage 2 National Curriculum for Years 3 and 4. They can also be used for older pupils with less-well developed language skills.

How to use this Book

Understanding & Using Spoken Language is divided into three main sections: 'Understanding Spoken Language'; 'Using Spoken Language' and 'Teaching Resources'. The first two sections are each subdivided into three different skill areas. There are 24 activities in each skill area, in four ability stages, Stage I – Stage IV, Stage I being the easiest and Stage IV the hardest.

We have designed the activities to fit into the existing curriculum as far as possible. The tabs down the side of each page suggest which areas of the curriculum best suit that particular activity, and also indicate the ability stage.

Each activity includes a clear aim, the equipment and preparation required, clear instructions and, where appropriate, additional tips and ways of extending the activity. There is an extensive Teaching Resources section containing texts and some pictures to be used with specific activities. Equipment and preparation has been kept to a minimum, but where it is necessary this is clearly indicated.

The games are grouped in Stages I-IV, from easy to harder. The Stages do not correspond rigidly to ages, but progress broadly along developmental lines. It is very difficult to ensure that the activities follow each other in small developmental steps. In some cases the move from one stage to the next may involve a considerable increase in difficulty. The authors also recognise that a number of the activities in Stages 3 and 4 are quite challenging for Year 4 pupils. They feel it is as important to offer material which will stretch the most linguistically able children, as it is to establish sound foundations for all children. Activities should be chosen to match the needs and abilities of the children involved.

Although the authors have made reference to the National Curriculum of England and Wales, the activities are not dependent on knowledge or experience of the National Curriculum and can be carried out by any English-speaking user. (See 'Notes for Users Outside the UK' below.)

In addition, each section includes two brief 'warm-up' activities, which are intended to take only a few minutes. You may wish to choose one or both of these to set the scene, and focus the pupils prior to the main activity.

THE SKILL AREAS

Understanding Spoken Language

▲ *Active Listening and Memory*
Activities to promote careful listening for content, ambiguity and inconsistency and memory for facts.

▲ *Thinking and Reasoning*
Activities to encourage the use of language to identify and solve problems.

▲ *Word Play*
Activities to develop the appreciation of word characteristics such as alliteration and onomatopoeia, and groups of words such as homonyms, homophones and antonyms.

Using Spoken Language

▲ *Explaining and Describing*
Activities to develop pupils' ability to give clear and accurate explanations and descriptions.

▲ *Reporting and Debating*
Activities that develop the skills needed for clear verbal reporting, and which offer opportunities for discussion, dissent and debate.

▲ *Using Speech Effectively*
These activities are aimed at developing clarity of speech, and the use of intonation, speed, pace and rhythm.

ESTABLISHING STARTING LEVELS

The games are grouped in Stages I–IV, from easy to harder. Stage I is likely to be the preferred starting point for children at the beginning of Year 3 (seven to eight years). As with any activity, there will be considerable variation in the children's abilities, and different groups of children can be moved on through the stages at their own speed. More linguistically able children are likely to have completed Stage IV before the end of Year 4 (eight to nine year olds).

TARGET-SETTING

The activities are designed to support mainstream pupils in attaining National Curriculum targets for Speaking and Listening. However, you may have children in your class who have Individual Education Plans. Many of the activities could be used as part of the Individual Education Plan (IEP) target-setting process, as have activities from the authors' previous book, *Games for Speaking, Listening and Understanding*. Each activity has a particular aim, which is worded in accordance with target-setting protocol.

RECORD-KEEPING

There are optional record-keeping forms to enable you to monitor progress. These are divided into 'Understanding Spoken Language' and 'Using Spoken Language'. The names of the children are entered in the left-hand column. A key suggesting how progress is recorded appears at the top of each form. Using the forms in this way will indicate individual children's strengths and weaknesses, and so aid in future planning.

NOTES FOR USERS OUTSIDE THE UK

◆ The National Curriculum of England and Wales provides a statutory entitlement to learning for all pupils. It provides a syllabus for all subjects, with clearly stated attainment targets and a structure for monitoring progress.

◆ 'Circle Time' refers to whole-group teaching sessions where the teacher leads a variety of activities to promote listening skills, group interaction and social communication skills.

◆ The 'Literacy Hour' is a structured approach to teaching basic literacy skills to children between the ages of five and 11 years.

It is divided into word, sentence and text levels, thereby addressing phonics, grammar and creative writing skills.

◆ The 'Numeracy Hour' is a structured approach to teaching mathematics and number skills.

◆ In the Teaching Resources, UK currency occurs within some activities. If necessary, alter the currency to match that of the user's country. The same applies to mention of specific sports teams.

ACTIVE LISTENING & MEMORY

ACTIVE LISTENING & MEMORY

Warm-Ups for Active Listening

Earth and Sky

Each person needs to stand in a space with their feet facing forward, about a shoulders' width apart. Stand in front of the group so that everyone can see you. Start with your right hand in front of you, palm facing inwards level with your waist. Your left hand is at waist level, in front of you, palm facing down. Slowly move your right hand up past your face then turn your palm up as if pushing up the sky. At the same time, push down with your left hand. Hold for a second, then twist your right hand so that the palm faces in again, and slowly bring it down past your face. At the same time your left hand comes up to push up the sky. Your hands should pass each other at about chest level, with the left hand on the inside. This sounds really complicated, but it is actually simple and graceful, and can be repeated as many times as you wish. It is good for calming down and focusing one's thinking.

Grant's Game

This is a counting game. The group stand in a circle, and the first person starts to count. They can say as many numbers as they wish, up to five. The next person counts on, keeping to the 'maximum of five rule'. The person who has to say 20 is out, and they sit down. The winner is the last person left standing. Children quickly learn how to 'work' the counting to make sure they are not out. You can alter the criteria – for example, stopping at 10 and only allowing counts of one or two.

ACTIVE LISTENING ⁂ MEMORY

Stage I
Stage II
Stage III
Stage IV
Circle Time
Hall/PE
Literacy
Numeracy
Drama
Small Group
Art
Humanities
Science
Design Technology
PHSE
Food Technology

Greetings Card

Aim
To be able to follow instructions to make a simple greetings card.

Equipment

Drawing equipment, card, and a selection of decorative materials.

Preparation

You will need to decide what sort of card it is to be, and jot down the basic instructions for making it. (See examples below.)

Activity

Explain to the children that they are each going to make a card. Tell them what the occasion is, and who the card might be for. Each child should be able to reach the materials easily. They must listen carefully, and try to do exactly what you tell them. Sometimes they will need to choose their own colour, and at other times they must use the colour you suggest. Read each part of the instruction twice before anyone is allowed to start. Allow the children to complete each instruction before giving the next. At the end you can check that everyone has added all the decorations and details you suggested.

Example

A birthday card for Gran
Fold your piece of card in half.
Draw a big flower on the front of the card.
Colour the petals red or yellow.
Choose four shiny sequins from the box.
Stick one sequin in each corner on the front of the card.
Open up the card.
Choose a piece of coloured tissue-paper from the box.
Cut it into a flower shape.
Stick it on the right-hand page.
Write 'To Gran' at the top.
Write 'Love from, and then your name', in red under the flower.

Stage I

Stage II

Stage III

Stage IV

Circle Time

Hall/PE

Literacy

Numeracy

Drama

Small Group

Art

Humanities

Science

Design Technology

PHSE

Food Technology

ACTIVE LISTENING & MEMORY

Harriet's Hats

Aim
To be able to follow instructions relating to pattern and colour.

Equipment

'Harriet's Hats' template from Teaching Resources (page 162).

Preparation

Write simple descriptions of seven different hats, one for every day of the week. Write the descriptions on a large sheet of paper. Mark which hat refers to which day (see examples below). Copy the hat template for each child.

How to Play

Give each child a 'Harriet's Hats' sheet, and a supply of colouring pencils or crayons. Tell them that Harriet loves hats and wears a different one every day of the week. Describe the first hat, and give them time to colour it according to your description. Continue until all the hats are coloured. Now the children must cut out the individual hats, following the dotted lines. They should write their initials on their hats. You can then collect all the hats and shuffle them. Put the sheet with the descriptions of the hats up so that everyone can see it. Ask a child to pick a hat from the pile, and see if they can identify which day it belongs to by its colour and pattern.

Example

On Mondays Harriet liked to wear the white hat with purple spots.
On Tuesdays she always wore the red hat with the black feather.
On Wednesdays the green and yellow stripy hat was her favourite.
Thursday was the blue and white check hat's turn.
Friday was market day, so she wore the yellow hat with an orange bow.
On Saturday she went to watch football, wearing the green hat with black stars.
On Sundays she always wore the pink and blue stripy hat.

ACTIVE LISTENING & MEMORY

Stage I

Stage II

Stage III

Stage IV

Circle Time

Hall/PE

Literacy

Numeracy

Drama

Small Group

Art

Humanities

Science

Design Technology

PHSE

Food Technology

Waiter!

Aim

To be able to remember a list of instructions.

Equipment

Food pictures from Teaching Resources (page 163).

Preparation

Copy two sets of the food pictures, and cut them up into individual pictures.

Activity

Separate the children into three or more small groups, sitting at separate tables. Choose someone to be a waiter, and someone to be the chef. Put one food picture onto each table, which the 'diners' look at and then turn face down. Lay out the second complete set in front of the chef. The waiter then visits three or more tables and takes their orders, which will be the items on their concealed pictures. He goes to the chef, tells him what has been ordered, (three or more items) collects the appropriate pictures, and takes the orders back to each table. The 'diners' check to see if they have the right order. Then change both waiter and chef, and give out another set of orders. Repeat the activity as often as time permits.

Example

An apple. A glass of cola. An iced bun.

Tip

You can make the memory load harder by letting each table order two or more items.

Extension

Children could suggest different food items, and make the pictures using a computer graphics programme. Menu cards could be made in Design and Technology. Add a bit of fun by allowing the 'diners' to criticise their orders – for example, burnt, undercooked, no chips – and getting the waiter to relay the criticisms to the chef.

Stage I

Stage II

Stage III

Stage IV

Circle Time

Hall/PE

Literacy

Numeracy

Drama

Small Group

Art

Humanities

Science

Design Technology

PHSE

Food Technology

ACTIVE LISTENING ⚹ MEMORY

Railway Stations

Aim
To be able to remember and spot the instruction that applies to you.

Equipment

None.

Activity

Seat the children one behind the other in a long line, on chairs, a bench, or the floor.
Explain that they are on a train. At every station there are people on the platform selling things to eat and drink. Each child will be told what they are allowed to buy, and when the train stops at a station where those things are being sold, they can get off the train. Decide on four different types of refreshment. Tell the first four children what they can buy – for example, apples, chocolate, orange squash, ice-cream. Repeat the same sequence for the next four and so on, until everyone knows their snack. Then set the train going, and talk about its journey, without making the instructions too clear or direct. ('The train is slowing down for Notown. I can see the man coming along the platform. I think he has a tray of chocolate.') The children who were told they could buy chocolate get off the train, with or without reminders. Set the train going again. ('Right, off we go again. The next station is quite soon. Oh yes, here we are – there is a man selling lovely ripe apples and pears.') The game ends when everybody has got off the train.

Extension

Make it harder by 'wrapping up' the instructions – for example, 'There's a man selling lollipops and *chocolate* and mugs of coffee.'

ACTIVE LISTENING
& MEMORY

Give it a Name

Aim

To be able to think of a suitable title for a short story.

Equipment

'Give it a Name' texts from Teaching Resources (page 164).

Activity

Explain to the children that you are going to read them a very short story. The author has given it a name, but the publisher does not like what has been chosen. The children are to think up a better title. Read the text a couple of times, and then ask for suggestions for good titles. These could be written up, or recorded on to audiotape. Then go through the various suggestions, asking for a show of hands to vote on the suitability of each one. The most popular title is chosen for the story.

Extension

The children could continue the story as a creative writing activity, or produce a different story to match the chosen title.

When you have used all the texts in Teaching Resources, go over the titles chosen again. Can the children remember which story went with which title?

Stage I

Stage II

Stage III

Stage IV

Circle Time

Hall/PE

Literacy

Numeracy

Drama

Small Group

Art

Humanities

Science

Design Technology

PHSE

Food Technology

Stage I

Stage II

Stage III

Stage IV

Circle Time

Hall/PE

Literacy

Numeracy

Drama

Small Group

Art

Humanities

Science

Design Technology

PHSE

Food Technology

ACTIVE LISTENING & MEMORY

Fill in the Gaps

Aim
To be able to see when instructions are not adequate to enable the task to be carried out, and to ask for clarification or further details.

Equipment

None.

Preparation

Jot down a selection of incomplete or confusing instructions, including some with unfamiliar vocabulary. (See examples below.)

Activity

Tell the children you are going to give each of them in turn an instruction. You may have left something out, or there may be unknown words in it, or some other source of confusion. Their job is to tell you what you need to add or change, so that they can carry out the task.

Examples

'Put it on my table', (Child: 'Put what on your table?' Teacher: 'Oh, sorry, a pencil from your desk'.)
'Put your book on top' ('On top of what?')
'Get one out of the cupboard.' ('One what?')
'Take the book to Miss X.' ('You haven't given me a book.')
'Go and stand by Jack.' ('Which Jack? There are two in the class.')
'Share your storybook with Kitty.' ('Kitty is away today.')
'Put your pencil away in the *armoire*.' ('Please, I don't know what an *armoire* is.')

Tip

You might make this more of a challenge by including a few instructions which are complete and unambiguous, so that the children have to listen more carefully, and can also have more fun by catching you out.

ACTIVE LISTENING ⟋ MEMORY

Stage I

Stage II

Stage III

Stage IV

Circle Time

Hall/PE

Literacy

Numeracy

Drama

Small Group

Art

Humanities

Science

Design Technology

PHSE

Food Technology

Mrs Chatter's Shopping

Aim

To be able to extract the important information from a wordy message.

Equipment

Toy food items, or pictures of familiar food and household items.

Preparation

Jot down what you are going to say. (See examples below.)

Activity

Choose a child to be the first shopkeeper, and put the shopping items out in front of him. The children are all going to take turns to do Mrs Chatter's shopping for her. You will be Mrs Chatter, and give the first child a long-winded message. The child goes to the shop and asks for the items 'hidden' in the message. That child then becomes the shopkeeper, and the next child is given a 'shopping list', and so on until everybody has had a turn.

Examples

1 'Good morning my dear, isn't it just a perfect day, I can't wait to get out into my garden. Now let's see what I need from the shop. Oh yes, that cat of mine is a greedy boy; he's finished all his tins of cat food, so I need three of those. And Mr Jones is coming round for tea, so you'd better get me a packet of his favourite biscuits too.'
2 'It is good of you to do my shopping. I want to wash those big curtains in my living room and I've run out of washing powder – and I do believe its warm enough to do some gardening, so you could get me a packet of sunflower seeds as well?'

Tips

Have plenty more items than the children can buy, or replace the items after each turn, so that the children cannot just use a process of elimination. Make sure the items you mention actually exist in the 'shop'!

ACTIVE LISTENING & MEMORY

Stage I

Stage II

Stage III

Stage IV

Circle Time

Hall/PE

Literacy

Numeracy

Drama

Small Group

Art

Humanities

Science

Design Technology

PHSE

Food Technology

Character Sketch

Aim
To extract sufficient information from a text to be able to make a drawing.

Equipment

Two of the 'Character Sketch' texts from Teaching Resources (page 165).
Counters or cubes in two different colours to represent the two different characters.
Drawing materials.

How to Play

Each child will need some paper, and drawing and colouring equipment. Explain that you are going to read them a description of two different characters. They will need to listen carefully because when you have finished reading they are going to try to draw the characters. Read the first text twice. After the second reading the children are given time to do a quick drawing. Repeat with the second text. Now clear a space on the floor so that all the pictures can be laid out. Give each child a counter or cube of each colour. Remind them which colour represents which character, and then tell them to put their counters or cubes on two of the matching character pictures. (Not their own!)

ACTIVE LISTENING ‡ MEMORY

Stage I

Stage II

Stage III

Stage IV

Circle Time

Hall/PE

Literacy

Numeracy

Drama

Small Group

Art

Humanities

Science

Design Technology

PHSE

Food Technology

What were they Doing?

Aim

To be able to identify the main thrust of a brief story, and not be distracted by detail.

Equipment

'What were they Doing?' stories from Teaching Resources (pages 166–167).

Preparation

Copy as many of the stories as there are children taking part. (This game is probably best for not more than six or so.) Write down the name of the character in each story on separate slips of paper and put them in a bag or box.

Activity

Choose a child to pick out one of the slips. This will tell you which story to begin with, and the child who chose it has to listen especially carefully, as they will be the one to answer your question at the end. Then choose another child to pick a slip. Read the next story, and repeat until everyone has had a turn.

Example

Jemma badly needed a new dress for the party. She stood and looked in the shop window for ages. There were such beautiful things in it! There was a long red dress with frilly sleeves, and a pretty blue one with stars on it. Jemma wondered if she had enough money for either of them, as she had spent a lot on her holiday in America recently. She looked at her watch, and realised it was nearly time for the bus. 'I'll just have to make up my mind', she thought, and pushed open the door.
Question: What was Jemma doing?
Answer: Shopping for a party dress.
Some typical wrong answers might be: Standing outside a shop, waiting for the bus.

Stage I

Stage II

Stage III

Stage IV

Circle Time

Hall/PE

Literacy

Numeracy

Drama

Small Group

Art

Humanities

Science

Design Technology

PHSE

Food Technology

ACTIVE LISTENING & MEMORY

Word Alert (1)

Aim
To be able to pick out specific words in spoken language.

Equipment

'Word Alert (1)' texts from Teaching Resources (pages 168–169).
Pencils and paper.

Activity

Give each child a pencil and a sheet of paper. Tell them they have to listen to a short story and put a tick on their sheet every time they hear an action word. You will have to explain what you mean by action words, and let them practise, by using the example below. Read each little story twice. The children are not allowed to mark the paper until the second reading. Then tell them to count the number of ticks and write the number on the sheet. Ask for hands up for the maximum number of ticks, and work down until you reach the lowest number.

Example

Sam *climbed* on top of the gate. He *jumped* down onto the grass, and *ran* across the field. When he got to the tree he *flopped* down on the ground, exhausted. After a few minutes he *staggered* to his feet and *leant* against the tree trunk. (6 points.)

ACTIVE LISTENING & MEMORY

Stage I

Stage II

Stage III

Stage IV

Circle Time

Hall/PE

Literacy

Numeracy

Drama

Small Group

Art

Humanities

Science

Design Technology

PHSE

Food Technology

Whose Birthday?

Aim
To be able to work out the recipient from a verse in a card.

Equipment

Birthday card verses from Teaching Resources (page 170). Old greetings cards (optional).

Preparation

Make a copy of the sheet of verses. You may like to make the activity more realistic by sticking the verses inside old greetings cards. Write the following recipients on cards: Mum, Dad, Granny, Grandad, Auntie, Uncle, Brother, Sister, Cousin, Friend.

Activity

This activity is suitable for up to eight children. Give each child a recipient card. Help them read the names on the cards. Tell them you have a pile of birthday cards, but you do not know who they are for because there are no addresses on the envelopes. The only way you can work out who they are for is by reading the verse inside the card. Read the first verse, and the child who thinks it is for them holds up the recipient card. If they are right, give them the verse or card. Continue until everyone has a card.

Stage I

Stage II

Stage III

Stage IV

Circle Time

Hall/PE

Literacy

Numeracy

Drama

Small Group

Art

Humanities

Science

Design Technology

PHSE

Food Technology

ACTIVE LISTENING & MEMORY

Commercials

Aim

To be able to work out what product is being advertised in promotional material.

Equipment

'Commercials' from Teaching Resources (page 171).

Preparation

Copy the list of commercials for yourself.

Activity

Divide the children into two teams. Explain that you are going to start reading out the words of a commercial. As soon as anyone thinks they know what is being advertised, they must put up their hand. (If at all possible, supply the players with buzzers or small noise makers, as it is easier for you to spot who has responded first if you can hear them buzz or ring a bell, than to see which hand was up first). If the first child to respond has got the answer right, their team wins two points. If not, continue reading until somebody gets the right answer, when their team is awarded one point. If nobody gets it, continue reading to the end, when the product is revealed.

Example

'It's the new superfast, safe and comfortable way to travel. It's sleek and streamlined, quiet and smooth. It corners without you noticing it, and you won't even see your glass shake. London to Manchester in two hours 10 minutes, this is the transport of the future: the new Supatrain!'

ACTIVE LISTENING ≠ MEMORY

	Stage I
	Stage II
	Stage III
	Stage IV
	Circle Time
	Hall/PE
	Literacy
	Numeracy
	Drama
	Small Group
	Art
	Humanities
	Science
	Design Technology
	PHSE
	Food Technology

Stop Thief!

Aim
To be able to listen for, and remember, specific pieces of information.

Equipment

'Stop Thief!' mini-stories in Teaching Resources (page 172).

Preparation

Copy one or more of the mini-stories for yourself.

Activity

This game can be played either by individuals or in small teams. Explain to the children that you are going to read them a mini-story about a thief. You will ask each child or group to listen out for certain pieces of information. At the end of the story, ask each child or group what information they will be able to give to the police.

Example

One person or group to listen out for: the appearance of the thief; the name of the shop being robbed; what kind of shop it was; the registration number of the getaway car; the appearance of any witnesses; the time of day, and what the weather was like.

Stage I

Stage II

Stage III

Stage IV

Circle Time

Hall/PE

Literacy

Numeracy

Drama

Small Group

Art

Humanities

Science

Design Technology

PHSE

Food Technology

ACTIVE LISTENING & MEMORY

Poetry Please

Aim

To be able to work out what is being described in a piece of verse.

Equipment

Short verses from Teaching Resources (pages 173–175).

Preparation

Copy and cut out enough verses for either the individual children or small groups taking part. Keep a copy of the whole list of verses for yourself, with the answers in case you are in any doubt!

Activity

Give each child or group a verse, turned face down on the table. If the children are playing in groups, each group must appoint a reader who, on the command 'Go!', turns the slip of paper over and reads out the verse. As soon as a child or group thinks they know what the verse is about, they should put their hands up. Check for correctness, and then ask the individual or a group member to read the verse out to the rest of the class. Give every child or group a turn to read out their verse and say what it is about. The quickest child or group is the winner.

Example

It runs like a silver ribbon
Whispering over the weeds.
The willows bend over its ripples
As it winds between the reeds.
Answer: stream or river.

ACTIVE LISTENING & MEMORY

Word Alert (2)

Aim
To be able to pick out specific words in spoken language.

Equipment

'Word Alert (2)' texts from Teaching Resources (pages 176–177).
Pencils and paper.

Activity

Give each child a pencil and a sheet of paper. Tell them you are going to read a short story, and they have to listen for all the adjectives, putting a tick on their paper each time they hear one. You may need to explain that adjectives are describing words, and let them practise by using the example below. Read each little story twice. The children are not allowed to mark the paper until the second reading. Then tell them to count the number of ticks and write the number on the sheet. Ask for hands up for the maximum number of ticks, and work down until you reach the lowest number.

Example

The sun beat down on the *burning* rocks. In the distance the *blue* hills shimmered in the heat. There was an *eerie* silence. Just beyond the rocks was an *ancient, twisted* tree. Underneath the tree sat a man. He had a *long* beard, and was wearing a *moth-eaten* cloak. In his hand he held a *sharp, glittering* dagger. (9 points)

Stage I
Stage II
Stage III
Stage IV
Circle Time
Hall/PE
Literacy
Numeracy
Drama
Small Group
Art
Humanities
Science
Design Technology
PHSE
Food Technology

ACTIVE LISTENING & MEMORY

Stage I

Stage II

Stage III

Stage IV

Circle Time

Hall/PE

Literacy

Numeracy

Drama

Small Group

Art

Humanities

Science

Design Technology

PHSE

Food Technology

Tombola

Aim

To be able to remember several numbers for up to five minutes.

Equipment

A random collection of numbers on slips of paper placed in a container. (There must be enough slips for each child to have one.) A list of four or five prizes, with numbers allocated to them (for example: No 1 A Skateboard; No 2 A box of chocolates; No 3 The latest must-have book; No 4 A ticket to the pantomime; No 5 A digital camera).

Activity

Explain that you are going to have a pretend tombola. One by one the children pull a number out of the container. When they have all drawn a number and memorised it, the slips go back into the container. You then tell the children what the four or five prizes are – that is No 1 A skateboard, No 2 A box of chocolates, and so on – stressing that it is important to remember them. Now promote a few minutes' conversation about tombolas, what prizes the children may have won in the past, which of the pretend prizes they would most like to win, and why. After four or five minutes, get a child to draw the first number out of the container and read it out. Who does it belong to? If it is correctly claimed, and has a prize allocated to it, the owner of the winning ticket can 'choose' his prize – *provided* he can remember what number the prize is!

Extension

You could set this game up at the beginning of a lesson and draw the tickets at the end of the lesson, or set it up on one day and draw the tickets the next day, thus stretching the children's memories.
You could 'auction' unclaimed prizes at the end.

ACTIVE LISTENING ⟡ MEMORY

Get Organised!

Aim
To be able to listen and record information accurately.

Equipment

'Get Organised!' template and texts from Teaching Resources (pages 178–179).

Preparation

Give each child a copy of the template and a supply of pencils and pencil crayons.

Activity

The class is divided into reds, blues, greens and yellows. Children draw round the edge of one oval on the template in their group colour. Now tell the children you are going to read them some instructions. They must try to record the information that applies to their group in their coloured oval. They can use quick drawings or write single words. The instructions will be read twice. The first time they must just listen, the second time they can record the information.

Stage I

Stage II

Stage III

Stage IV

Circle Time

Hall/PE

Literacy

Numeracy

Drama

Small Group

Art

Humanities

Science

Design Technology

PHSE

Food Technology

ACTIVE LISTENING & MEMORY

Stage I

Stage II

Stage III

Stage IV

Circle Time

Hall/PE

Literacy

Numeracy

Drama

Small Group

Art

Humanities

Science

Design Technology

PHSE

Food Technology

Calendar

Aim
To be able to extract information from a spoken text.

Equipment

'Calendar' template and texts from Teaching Resources (pages 180–181).

Preparation

Make a copy of the 'Calendar' template for each child.

Activity

Give out the copies of the calendar template. Tell the children that you are going to read an extract from a diary. They will hear some dates, which they must mark on the calendar. Explain that they can mark the date with a word or a quick picture. You may like to have a discussion about the kinds of pictures – for example, swimming can be indicated by drawing a wavy line. You then read the text once and everyone listens. On the second reading they mark their calendars. When you have finished, ask questions to check that they have recorded the information correctly.

ACTIVE LISTENING + MEMORY

Ask Me a Question

Aim
To be able to ask a relevant question as a result of listening.

Equipment

'Ask Me a Question' texts from Teaching Resources (pages 182–184).
Paper and pencils for making notes.

Activity

Tell the children you are going to read them part of a story. Explain that it is a mystery story, and there will be a lot of information missing. Divide the children into pairs or threes, and appoint a scribe in each group. They have to listen carefully to the story and think of a question they want answered. Read the story twice. On the second reading they should start thinking about their questions. When you have finished reading, allow them about a minute to agree on their question and to write it down. A spokesperson from each group then asks their group's question. Write the questions on the whiteboard. There is likely to be some duplication of questions. You can then answer the questions outright, or invite discussion as to possible answers.

Extension

Following the activity, the children could write their own versions of the story.

Stage I

Stage II

Stage III

Stage IV

Circle Time

Hall/PE

Literacy

Numeracy

Drama

Small Group

Art

Humanities

Science

Design Technology

PHSE

Food Technology

Stage I

Stage II

Stage III

Stage IV

Circle Time

Hall/PE

Literacy

Numeracy

Drama

Small Group

Art

Humanities

Science

Design Technology

PHSE

Food Technology

ACTIVE LISTENING & MEMORY

Word Alert (3)

Aim
To be able to pick out specific words in spoken language.

Equipment

'Word Alert (3)' texts from Teaching Resources (pages 185–186).
Pencils and paper.

Activity

Give each child a pencil and sheet of paper. Tell them you are going to read a short story, and they have to listen for all the words or phrases referring to time, putting a tick on their paper for each one they spot. You will need to explain what you mean by time words – use the example below for practice. Read each little story twice. The children are not allowed to mark the paper until the second reading. Then tell them to count the number of ticks and write the number on the sheet. Ask for hands up for the maximum number of ticks, and work down until you reach the lowest number.

Example

Early on Saturday morning there was a knock at the door. *When* Josh opened the door there was nobody there. *Then* he heard a sound. He looked at the path beside the front door. There was a box on the path. There it was *again*, a little squeak, coming from the box. *Then* silence. *After a while* Josh walked over to the box. (6 points)

Speechmark

ACTIVE LISTENING ≉ MEMORY

Stage I

Stage II

Stage III

Stage IV

Circle Time

Hall/PE

Literacy

Numeracy

Drama

Small Group

Art

Humanities

Science

Design Technology

PHSE

Food Technology

Story Map

Aim
To be able to record information in note form.

Equipment

'Story Map' template and texts from Teaching Resources (pages 187–190).
Acetate overlays and thin dry-wipe pens if possible.

Preparation

Make a copy of the template for each child. If possible give each child an acetate overlay and a dry-wipe pen. If not you will need to make additional copies of the template, one for each story.

Activity

Tell the children you are going to read some little stories. Explain that they can record *'who'*, *'where'* and *'what'* information on their 'Story Map' sheet. Go through the practice story, recording the information in pictures on the sheet. Then see if anyone can use the sheet to retell the story. You are now ready to read the first story. Explain that you will read it twice. On the first reading the children must just listen. The second time you read it they can start to record the information.

ACTIVE LISTENING & MEMORY

Stage I

Stage II

Stage III

Stage IV

Circle Time

Hall/PE

Literacy

Numeracy

Drama

Small Group

Art

Humanities

Science

Design Technology

PHSE

Food Technology

No!

Aim
To be able to spot contradictions in reported material.

Equipment

'No!' short 'news' paragraphs from Teaching Resources (page 191).

Preparation

Copy a selection of 'news' paragraphs to read out.

Activity

Explain to the children that you are going to read a short 'newspaper' item to them. Somewhere in it there will be a contradiction – something that cannot be true. Can they spot it? If anyone thinks they have identified the 'fact' that cannot be true, they must put up their hand. If there is more than one hand up, continue to take suggestions until either no more ideas are offered, or they have identified the suspect item. Play this as a game in which the children are pitted against you, the 'reporter'. Suppose you read out six paragraphs – can they spot your error three times or more?

Example

The Sludgy Canal clearing project today reported a great success. A long stretch has been re-opened to shipping. This stretch includes several 6m high bridges, a watermill, and a lock. The first yacht in 30 years to navigate this canal tied up at Maltings Mill on Tuesday afternoon. She is the yacht *Bluebell*, a 25m long bermuda-rigged boat with a 10m mast.

ACTIVE LISTENING & MEMORY

For and Against

Aim
To be able to identify the speaker's opinion on a certain topic.

Equipment

'For and Against' texts from Teaching Resources (pages 193–194).
Blank sheets of paper (scrap paper will do).

Activity

Explain to the children that you are going to read some pieces of text. They need to listen carefully and decide whether the writer of the text is for or against the proposition. Tell them to write FOR and AGAINST at the top of their sheet of paper. Read the text twice. After the second reading the children have to put a tick under the FOR or AGAINST column. You may like to read several texts and then go back and discuss the children's findings, or deal with each one as it occurs. You can add your own text linked to specific areas of the curriculum – for example, PHSE.

Stage I
Stage II
Stage III
Stage IV
Circle Time
Hall/PE
Literacy
Numeracy
Drama
Small Group
Art
Humanities
Science
Design Technology
PHSE
Food Technology

ACTIVE LISTENING & MEMORY

Stage I

Stage II

Stage III

Stage IV

Circle Time

Hall/PE

Literacy

Numeracy

Drama

Small Group

Art

Humanities

Science

Design Technology

PHSE

Food Technology

Training Sessions

Aim
To be able to identify a job or profession from the attributes needed to do it.

Equipment

'Training Sessions' list of jobs and attributes from Teaching Resources (page 195).

Preparation

Copy the list of jobs and attributes for yourself.

Activity

Tell the children that you are going to give them some idea of the qualities needed for certain jobs and professions. They have to try to guess what the job is. Some qualities are needed for several different jobs, and these are included deliberately to make things more difficult. You then read out the qualities required for a particular job, one at a time, or choose a child to read. As soon as somebody thinks they can identify the job, they put their hand up. If they are right, the game moves on to the next job. If they are wrong, the reader continues with his list until the job is correctly guessed.

Example

Good balance. Likes working on his own. Good head for heights. Good with his hands. Strong. Agile. (Steeplejack)

THINKING & REASONING

Stage I

Stage II

Stage III

Stage IV

Circle Time

Hall/PE

Literacy

Numeracy

Drama

Small Group

Art

Humanities

Science

Design Technology

PHSE

Food Technology

THINKING & REASONING

Warm-Ups for Thinking Skills

Marching
Everyone stands in a space. Stand in front of the children so that they can all see you. Raise your left hand and right foot, lower them and raise right hand and left foot. Keep doing this counting 'one' as you raise them, 'two' as you lower them. It is easy once you get into a rhythm, but you need to practise first! Some children find this very difficult at first, as it involves both sides of the brain. However, with practice they can improve, and it is thought to stimulate the brain to enable reasoning skills.

A to Z
Gather the children into a group. Starting with the letter 'A', go round the group and ask the children to think of something starting with each letter of the alphabet. The game can be played so that all the items have to be from one category.

THINKING & REASONING

Stage I

Stage II

Stage III

Stage IV

Circle Time

Hall/PE

Literacy

Numeracy

Drama

Small Group

Art

Humanities

Science

Design Technology

PHSE

Food Technology

Riddle-me-ree

Aim
To be able to work out the answer to easy riddles.

Equipment

List of riddles and answers from Teaching Resources (page 196).

Preparation

Write each riddle on a slip of paper.

Activity

Divide the children into two groups, and give each group an equal number of riddle slips to share out. The groups take turns to ask their opponents one of the riddles. The guessing team can confer. The winning group is the one which answers the most riddles correctly.

Example

What has a tail and can fly, but is not a bird? (Answer: A kite, aeroplane, dragonfly.)

Tip

Allow discussion, protest and dissent!

Stage I

Stage II

Stage III

Stage IV

Circle Time

Hall/PE

Literacy

Numeracy

Drama

Small Group

Art

Humanities

Science

Design Technology

PHSE

Food Technology

THINKING & REASONING

Rescue!

Aim

To be able to think out an appropriate response to a tricky situation.

Equipment

'Rescue' ideas for scenarios from Teaching Resources (page 197).

How to Play

Explain to the children that they are rescue workers, ready to help the police, the fire brigade, or the ambulance crew, and sometimes they will just have to cope on their own. You are going to tell them about a tricky situation they find themselves facing. Then you are going to suggest some ways they might deal with it. After each suggestion you will ask them for 'hands up' if they think that is a really good idea. Count the votes each time, and jot them down on the board or a piece of paper. At the end, tell them which idea gained the most votes. Then go on to the next scenario.

Examples

'A boy has fallen into a fast-flowing deep river, just near a bridge. It is quite a long way from the nearest house. There are lots of trees on the river banks. You saw a life-belt on the next bridge downstream.'
Would you: Jump in to try to save him?
Go and look for a phone?
Shout loudly?
Break off a branch from a tree and try to reach him with it?
Run to the next bridge and get the lifebelt?

Tip

It is worth encouraging some of the children to try to justify their choice of action. Foster debate within the group.

THINKING & REASONING

Stage I

Stage II

Stage III

Stage IV

Circle Time

Hall/PE

Literacy

Numeracy

Drama

Small Group

Art

Humanities

Science

Design Technology

PHSE

Food Technology

Links

Aim

To be able to identify ways in which unrelated objects or pictures have shared characteristics.

Equipment

The 'Raceboard' template from Teaching Resources (pages 198–199).
Counters, die and a collection of objects or object pictures (see examples below).

Preparation

If using objects, put them in a container. If using pictures, place them face down on the table.

Activity

This is a game for a group of not more than six children. Each player selects a coloured counter, and the first player throws the die. When a player lands on a star, they must take two objects out of the bag (or turn up two pictures from the table). They must then try to think of some way in which the two are related, and explain their idea. (This might be to do with function, components, material from which they are made, where they are found, and so on.) If they are successful they can move on two spaces. If not, they stay where they are. If a player lands on a sad face they go back one space, but if they land on a happy face, they go forward one space. You can make the game easier or harder by careful selection of the objects or pictures. An adult adjudicator is necessary.

Examples

Book, piece of paper, felt-tip pen, glove, sock, rubber, plastic dinosaur, toy car, spoon.

Tip

You can turn this into a large group or whole class activity by dispensing with the raceboard. Instead, hold up a series of object (or picture) pairs in front of the group, and ask for 'hands up' for suggestions as to possible links. You could also play it as a team game.

Stage I

Stage II

Stage III

Stage IV

Circle Time

Hall/PE

Literacy

Numeracy

Drama

Small Group

Art

Humanities

Science

Design Technology

PHSE

Food Technology

THINKING & REASONING

Thinking Pairs

Aim

To be able to share information with a partner, and together reach a solution to a puzzle.

Equipment

'Thinking Pairs' clue cards from Teaching Resources (page 200).

Preparation

Cut out the clue cards, keeping them in pairs. Select objects or pictures to match the answers, and put these on a table some distance from the children, covered with a cloth or concealed in some way.

Activity

Divide the children into pairs. Explain that each person in the pair will get a clue card. If they put their clues together and think about them, they will be able to find the object that matches their clues. Stand the children in two lines with the pairs opposite each other. Give out the linked clue cards. The first pair tell each other their clues (with help in reading if necessary), and go to the table to see if they can work out which object matches both their clues. Continue with the next pair of children, until everyone has had a turn.

THINKING & REASONING

Stage I

Stage II

Stage III

Stage IV

Circle Time

Hall/PE

Literacy

Numeracy

Drama

Small Group

Art

Humanities

Science

Design Technology

PHSE

Food Technology

Robot Challenge (1)

Aim
To be able to solve a problem using logical thinking.

Equipment

No equipment essential but a whistle or buzzer will help.

Preparation

Mark out an area called the 'Charging Station', and a separate area, directly opposite, called the 'Docking Station'. It will be helpful to have another adult to make sure everyone has moved in the correct way.

Activity

Label the children 1, 2 or 3. Make sure everyone can remember which number they are. Tell them that they are robots on a space station. Explain that they need to go to the Charging Station to charge their batteries, and to the Docking Station to wait for instructions from the astronauts. Then tell them how they can move, as follows:

1s can only move forwards in a straight line; 2s can only move sideways, to either side and 3s can only move backwards in a straight line. Line the children up in the Docking Station and tell them their batteries are low and need charging. Choose 1s, 2s or 3s to move to the Charging Station. Watch carefully to make sure they all move in the appropriate way. Sound the whistle or buzzer if anyone tries to cheat. Move the remaining groups in the same way.

Understanding & Using Spoken Language © C Delamain & J Spring 2004

Stage I

Stage II

Stage III

Stage IV

Circle Time

Hall/PE

Literacy

Numeracy

Drama

Small Group

Art

Humanities

Science

Design Technology

PHSE

Food Technology

THINKING & REASONING

Information Chain

Aim
To be able to identify an item from information already received.

Equipment

'Information Chain' list of objects and clues from Teaching Resources (page 201).

Preparation

Collect objects to match the clues. You need enough objects or pictures for every child in the group to have a chance to guess the answer. Copy and cut out the clues to make individual cards.

Activity

This is a game for not more than five children, sitting in a circle. Choose a selection of objects or pictures, and keep them hidden from sight. The idea is to give every child a separate clue. When all the clues are taken together, it is possible to work out the answer. Select one of the objects or pictures, and the relevant clue cards. Give each child a clue card. The first child reads out their clue. The next child repeats the first clue, and adds his own. Carry on in this way until you reach the last child, who, by this time, should be able to give the answer. If they cannot, allow others to offer a solution. Repeat the game with a different object or picture, and starting with a different player, until everyone in the group has had a go at guessing.

Examples

It is made of metal.
You keep it in the kitchen.
You use it at meal times.
You cannot cut with it.
You can eat cereal with it.

THINKING & REASONING

Explorers

Aim

To be able to work out what equipment might be useful in tricky situations.

Equipment

'Explorers' pictures from Teaching Resources (page 202).

Preparation

Copy and cut out the pictures, several of each.

Activity

Explain to the children that they are explorers, and have found themselves in difficult situations. Divide them into small groups of four or five, with one child in each as leader. Allocate a situation to each group. Tell the children that you have some things that might be useful, and give each group a good selection of both suitable and unsuitable equipment. Give the groups time to decide what items they might use and how. When everyone is ready, or after a set time, get each leader to explain how their group plans to get out of trouble. Encourage group discussion of their solutions, and exchange of equipment between groups, if necessary.

Examples

The explorers have come to: a river/a forest with no clear paths/a high wall with a tree beside, it but all the branches are high/up a place where the path has been washed away and there is a very steep drop/a dark tunnel entrance/a slippery slope/a deep snowdrift/some very tall grass that might have dangerous animals lurking in it/a place where there is danger of falling rocks/ a stretch of very narrow path, with a drop on one side and a cliff on the other/some swampy ground/some baking hot sand.

Tip

The children are not very likely to produce practical and well thought-out schemes. The value of this game lies in the discussion it generates.

Stage I
Stage II
Stage III
Stage IV
Circle Time
Hall/PE
Literacy
Numeracy
Drama
Small Group
Art
Humanities
Science
Design Technology
PHSE
Food Technology

Understanding & Using Spoken Language © C Delamain & J Spring 2004

THINKING & REASONING

Stage I

Stage II

Stage III

Stage IV

Circle Time

Hall/PE

Literacy

Numeracy

Drama

Small Group

Art

Humanities

Science

Design Technology

PHSE

Food Technology

Mysterious Meanings

Aim
To understand frequently used idioms.

Equipment

'Mysterious Meanings' list of idioms and possible meanings from Teaching Resources (page 203).

Preparation

Copy the list of idioms and possible meanings from Teaching Resources, and cut them out into individual slips.

Activity

Divide the group into teams of three. Give each team a slip with an idiom and its possible meaning written on it. Each team member must read out one of the three possible meanings of the idiom. The remaining teams – the audience – votes for which meaning they think is the correct one. Are they right? Repeat with the next team.

Examples

I am in deep water here.
(Options: 'I am out of my depth in the swimming pool'. 'I am drowning'. I am in a complicated situation that I don't know how to cope with'.)

You are too big for your boots.
(Options: 'You have outgrown your wellingtons.' 'The hiking boots you are trying on do not fit.' 'You are too self-confident and pleased with yourself'.)

THINKING & REASONING

Fact Finders

		Stage I
		Stage II
		Stage III
		Stage IV
		Circle Time
		Hall/PE
		Literacy
		Numeracy
		Drama
		Small Group
		Art
		Humanities
		Science
		Design Technology
		PHSE
		Food Technology

Aim

To be able to find information from a variety of sources.

Equipment

Reference books as follows: atlas; junior dictionary; natural history book; history book; books on space, human body, and plants.

'Fact Finders' question cards available from Teaching Resources (page 204).

Preparation

Arrange the reference books on a table. Copy and cut out the question cards into individual slips.

Activity

This is an activity for a group of up to 12 pupils. Divide the group into two. The children in the first group are given a book each, and the children in the second group are given a question card each. Give help with reading as necessary. Explain that each person with a question card has to try to find the person with the book which will contain their piece of information. When you say 'Go!' the children with the question cards move around trying to locate the right book. Once everyone has found their book, they can work in pairs to try to find the information asked for on their card.

Stage I

Stage II

Stage III

Stage IV

Circle Time

Hall/PE

Literacy

Numeracy

Drama

Small Group

Art

Humanities

Science

Design Technology

PHSE

Food Technology

THINKING & REASONING

Think Hard!

Aim
To be able to solve verbal maths problems.

Equipment

The Raceboard (page 198) and 'Think Hard!' cards from Teaching Resources (page 205).
A coloured counter for each player, and a die.

Preparation

Copy the problems onto card, and cut them out.

Activity

This activity is suitable for up to four players. Place the pile of cards beside the board. The first player rolls the die and moves the number of squares indicated. If they land on a star they take the top card from the pile. Give help with reading as necessary. If they can supply the right answer they get a bonus point. Any player landing on a sad face must go back one square. Any player landing on a happy face must go forward one square. The winner is the first to reach the end, but there will also be a 'thinking winner' – the player who collects the most bonus points.

THINKING & REASONING

Fit the Topic

Aim

To be able to identify the main theme of a spoken text.

Equipment

Simple symbols to represent the themes: forces, materials, nutrition, earth, sun, moon, electricity.
Statements taken from Year 3 or Year 4 Science topics, see example below.

Preparation

Place the symbols around the room, and write down the statements.

Activity

Divide the children into small groups of two, three or four depending, on how many children are involved. Make sure they understand what the various symbols represent. Choose a group to go first, and read them one of the statements. They must go to the part of the room indicated by the appropriate symbol, and stand by it.
Then read a text to the next group, and so on.
When every group has had a turn, repeat with some further texts.

Example

'It is the force that pulls things towards the earth. It is what makes things fall from heights, and what makes it harder to go up hill than down.'

Tip

Make sure the texts do not contain the crucial give-away words!

Stage I
Stage II
Stage III
Stage IV
Circle Time
Hall/PE
Literacy
Numeracy
Drama
Small Group
Art
Humanities
Science
Design Technology
PHSE
Food Technology

Stage I

Stage II

Stage III

Stage IV

Circle Time

Hall/PE

Literacy

Numeracy

Drama

Small Group

Art

Humanities

Science

Design Technology

PHSE

Food Technology

THINKING & REASONING

Robot Challenge (2)

Aim
To be able to solve a problem using logical thinking.

Equipment

None.

Activity

This is the same game as 'Robot Challenge (1)', (see page 37), but more complicated. Use the same basic criteria for moving, eg, forwards, backwards or sideways, but you can include some additional moves. Each child must make a quarter turn after every three steps. Instead of lining up the children opposite the area, have them standing facing in different directions.

THINKING &
REASONING

Stage I

Stage II

Stage III

Stage IV

Circle Time

Hall/PE

Literacy

Numeracy

Drama

Small Group

Art

Humanities

Science

Design Technology

PHSE

Food Technology

Sweetie Test

Aim
To be able to plan a fair test.

Equipment

A tube of sugar-coated chocolate beans of different colours, or other similar sweets.
A tape-measure or ruler.

Activity

Tell the children they are going to design a test to see if red chocolate beans roll further down a slope than the other colours. Divide the group into pairs or threes. Explain that they need to consider:

- **what equipment to use**
- **where the test will be done**
- **what they will need to measure**
- **how they will record the result.**

Each pair or three is given one of the above points to investigate. Allow them a few minutes to discuss their part of the investigation. Then bring the whole group together again. One child from each pair or three tells the rest of the group what they have planned. You will then need to collate all the information and check that there is agreement on the plan of action. Finally, carry out the test as planned by the children. If there are any serious flaws, there should be an opportunity to change the plan.

Extension

Devise additional 'Sweetie' problems so that the children are familiar with the idea of 'fair testing',
before they have to apply it in Science or Maths.
Examples might be:

- Do green sweets fall to the ground faster than pink ones?
- Are six orange sweets heavier than six yellow ones?
- Which sweet loses its colour first when dropped in water?

THINKING & REASONING

Stage I

Stage II

Stage III

Stage IV

Circle Time

Hall/PE

Literacy

Numeracy

Drama

Small Group

Art

Humanities

Science

Design Technology

PHSE

Food Technology

The Bridge

Aim
To be able to discuss and plan, cooperatively, how to make a structure that can hold a weight.

Equipment

Some newspapers.
Pairs of scissors.
A small weight, such as a rubber.

Activity

Divide the children into pairs or threes. Their task is to make a bridge between two supports – for example, between two piles of books. They can use one double sheet of newspaper and a pair of scissors. No other equipment is allowed, and the bridge has to be strong enough to support the chosen object. Any attempt, or change to an existing design, *must* be discussed and agreed on before it is tried.

THINKING & REASONING

	Stage I
	Stage II
	Stage III
	Stage IV
	Circle Time
	Hall/PE
	Literacy
	Numeracy
	Drama
	Small Group
	Art
	Humanities
	Science
	Design Technology
	PHSE
	Food Technology

Phone Call

Aim

To be able to listen to one side of a telephone conversation, and work out to whom the caller is talking.

Equipment

List of 'Phone call' conversations from Teaching Resources (page 206).

Preparation

Make a copy of the 'conversations' for yourself.

Activity

Tell the children you have been listening to somebody talking on the phone. Can they work out who is at the other end of the line? Act out the conversation, and at the end give them four options to choose from.

Example

'Have you had the stitches out yet?' (The plumber, the vet, someone who has had an operation, the dressmaker'.)

Extension

Play as above, but do not give the children any options.

THINKING & REASONING

Stage I

Stage II

Stage III

Stage IV

Circle Time

Hall/PE

Literacy

Numeracy

Drama

Small Group

Art

Humanities

Science

Design Technology

PHSE

Food Technology

Ferryboat

Aim
To solve a problem involving a process of elimination.

Equipment

'Ferryboat' game instructions and list of examples from Teaching Resources (page 207).

How to Play

Tell the children that they are going to play a game in which a ferryman takes passengers and goods across the river in his boat. He cannot take more than two at a time. Unfortunately he has to be very careful who he leaves alone on the bank. Suppose he leaves a wolf alone with a rabbit: the wolf might eat the rabbit. So he always has to decide who he should take first, and who he can safely leave alone together. Now choose a child to be the first ferryman. Choose children to take the roles of passengers and goods. If necessary, stick on labels to help the ferryman remember who or what they are. The ferryman then has to work out who he can take across the river safely without any harm coming to the remaining passengers or goods. Indicate the river with chalk marks, or by other means. Repeat with another example and different children.

Examples

A wolf, a rabbit, a crate of lettuces, a chicken and a sack of corn. (The wolf would eat the rabbit and the chicken; the rabbit would eat the lettuce; the chicken would eat the corn. The ferryman must take the rabbit and the chicken, as the wolf can be safely left with the lettuces and the corn.)

Tip

Introduce a bit of drama to this game. The ferryman can act rowing his passengers across the river. If he has made a mistake, the rabbit, for example, can act starting to eat the lettuces before the ferryman spots his error. Encourage discussion.

THINKING &
REASONING

Stage I

Stage II

Stage III

Stage IV

Circle Time

Hall/PE

Literacy

Numeracy

Drama

Small Group

Art

Humanities

Science

Design Technology

PHSE

Food Technology

Hidden Messages

Aim

To be able to decipher a simple code.

Equipment

'Code Key' template and message cards from Teaching Resources (pages 208–210).

Preparation

Copy and enlarge the Code Key. Copy and cut out the code cards and the message cards. Mark the back of the coded cards with an X. Leave the other message cards blank.

Activity

This activity is suitable for a small group, not exceeding six. Explain to the children that they are going to try to work out the meaning of some messages which are written in code. Display the key to the codes so that everyone can see it. The activity is like a pairs game. Lay out the two sets of cards. The first player takes one from each set of cards, and by referring to the key, tries to decide whether they are a pair or not. If they are, then that player keeps the pair. Continue until all the pairs have been claimed. The player with the most pairs is the winner.

THINKING & REASONING

Stage I

Stage II

Stage III

Stage IV

Circle Time

Hall/PE

Literacy

Numeracy

Drama

Small Group

Art

Humanities

Science

Design Technology

PHSE

Food Technology

Back to Back

Aim
To be able to work out differences by asking questions.

Equipment

Two identical sets of six everyday objects. Two trays and cloths to cover them.

Preparation

Put two rows of chairs back to back, with a table in front of each row. Put a set of objects on each tray and cover with a cloth.

Activity

Divide the group into two teams, A and B. The members of each team sit back to back on the chairs provided. Team A select three of the objects on their tray, and put the rest out of sight. The chosen objects are arranged on the tray. Team B uncover the objects on their tray. They then take turns to ask questions to find out which objects have been selected, and how they have been positioned on the tray. Make a note of the number of questions asked before Team B's tray looks identical to Team A's. Team B then takes the lead by selecting three objects and arranging them. The winner is the team who managed to match the objects by asking the fewest questions.

THINKING & REASONING

Stage I

Stage II

Stage III

Stage IV

Circle Time

Hall/PE

Literacy

Numeracy

Drama

Small Group

Art

Humanities

Science

Design Technology

PHSE

Food Technology

Alibis

Aim
To be able to spot the flaws in an alibi.

Equipment

'Alibi' texts and fact lists from Teaching Resources (pages 211–212).

Preparation

Copy enough different alibi texts to have one for each child playing, and enough copies of each associated fact list for the other players.

Activity

This is a game for not more than six children. Explain that everybody is going to have a turn to be a person accused of some crime. Choose somebody to go first, and give him his alibi. The rest of the group (the jury) is given the associated list of facts to study. The accused person then reads out his alibi. Some of the alibis are completely truthful, in which case the accused is acquitted. However, some contain one or more items which contradict the facts. Can the jury spot the part of the alibi which cannot be true? If they can, the accused is found guilty. The jury must wait until the accused has finished reading before challenging him.

Extension

Some children may be able to master their alibi well enough to make their plea without relying on the written word. You can also turn this game into a courtroom scene, in which one of the jurors becomes a prosecutor, and questions the accused.

THINKING & REASONING

Stage I

Stage II

Stage III

Stage IV

Circle Time

Hall/PE

Literacy

Numeracy

Drama

Small Group

Art

Humanities

Science

Design Technology

PHSE

Food Technology

Junk Designer

Aim
To think creatively about different ways in which objects could be used, and describe them.

Equipment

Raceboard (page 198) and the two sets of 'Junk Designer' cards from Teaching Resources (pages 213–214).
Coloured counters and a die.

Preparation

Make card copies of the 'Junk Designer' cards and cut them out. Divide them into two piles: the objects to be designed, and the 'junk'.

Activity

This is a game for a group of not more than six children. The aim of the game is to collect a 'design card' and a 'junk card', and see if it is possible to use the junk item to make the object. The players take turns to roll the die and move round the board. If a player lands on a star, they take a card from the pile. If they land on a sad face, they go back one space; if on a happy face, forward one space. When a child has one of each card, call out 'Design Time!' The players have to see if it is possible to use the junk item to make the object. All reasonable suggestions are acceptable. If they cannot think of any way of doing it, they return one or both cards to the bottom of their respective piles and start collecting again.

Extension

Use a supply of real junk, and give the children an opportunity to try to use their ideas, and make actual objects.

THINKING & REASONING

Who Wants to Know?

Aim

To be able to work out which question prompted a particular answer.

Equipment

'Who Wants to Know' list of questions and answers from Teaching Resources (page 215).

Preparation

Copy the questions and answers on to paper or card, and cut them out to make separate sets of 'Question' cards and 'Answer' cards.

Activity

This is a game for a maximum of 10 children. Give each child one of the 'Question' cards. If playing with fewer than 10 children, discard the spare 'Question' cards and their matching 'Answer' cards. Tell the children to read their questions, and check that they have understood and remembered them. You stand up, holding an 'Answer' card, and read it out. (Add a bit of drama if possible!) If any of the children can correctly claim that this is the answer to their question, they get a clap, and sit at the side. If nobody makes the connection immediately, the children come up to you in turn. Each time you read our your 'Answer', the child repeats his 'Question', and they and the group decide if the two go together. Continue until the right question is matched with your answer. If anybody is still unsure, repeat the procedure, but this time the children put their questions first, and you follow with the answer. This should make things clear. Continue with the other questions and answers.

Example

Answer: 'I'm sorry, I've only got a £5 note.'
Correct question: 'Excuse me, have you got any change for the parking meter?'
Incorrect question: 'Can you tell me when the last bus goes?'

Stage I

Stage II

Stage III

Stage IV

Circle Time

Hall/PE

Literacy

Numeracy

Drama

Small Group

Art

Humanities

Science

Design Technology

PHSE

Food Technology

Stage I

Stage II

Stage III

Stage IV

Circle Time

Hall/PE

Literacy

Numeracy

Drama

Small Group

Art

Humanities

Science

Design Technology

PHSE

Food Technology

THINKING & REASONING

Take Away

Aim
To be able to plan a meal taking into account the diners' dietary needs and preferences.

Equipment

'Take Away' menus and associated people from Teaching Resources (pages 216–217).

Preparation

Copy the menus and the lists of people that go with each one. Cut them out. Keep a copy of each menu and list of associated people for yourself.

Activity

Divide the children into groups of about four. Give each group a menu, and the list of people to accompany it. The task is to discuss and plan a meal, chosen from the options on the menu, that will be suitable for everyone on their list. The children should include one small dish, one main course, and one pudding. When everyone has had enough time, ask the group spokesmen to tell you what their diners are having. Give as much help as needed in explaining the various dishes and dietary requirements.

Menu:
Small dishes. Grapefruit. Tomato soup. Sardines. Small ham rolls and lettuce. Prawns and toast.

Examples

People:
Mrs Jones is allergic to shellfish. Mr Brown cannot eat any pork products. Miss Green and Mr Black can eat anything. Grapefruit, tomato soup, or sardines would be fine.

THINKING & REASONING

Stage I

Stage II

Stage III

Stage IV

Circle Time

Hall/PE

Literacy

Numeracy

Drama

Small Group

Art

Humanities

Science

Design Technology

PHSE

Food Technology

Sorted!

Aim

To grasp the core problem of a dilemma, and identify first steps towards solving it.

Equipment

List of 'Sorted!' dilemmas from Teaching Resources (page 218).

Preparation

Copy the 'dilemmas' list for yourself, and enough individual copies of each 'dilemma' for the number of small groups participating.

Activity

Explain to the children that you are going to present them with a series of dilemmas (problematic situations). The people concerned are rather muddle-headed, and cannot see where to start to solve their problems. The task is to work out what the core or most urgent difficulty is in each situation, and decide on the first essential step towards resolving it. The children may want to identify more than one step. Read out the first dilemma to the whole group. Now divide the children into sub-groups of between three and five, give them a copy of the dilemma, and allow them a few minutes to talk about it. Then ask the group spokesmen to tell you how they see the situation. Question the groups in turn until a reasonable appraisal is forthcoming. There may be more than one.

Example

Miss Showbiz wants to produce an amateur play this summer. There are only five people available who can really act. The best actress is away in May, and the best actor in September. Of three possible plays, one needs six good players, and one needs only four. Miss Showbiz does not want to upset anyone. The local hall has already been booked through July and August. The stage is quite small, and cannot accommodate a cast bigger than fourteen.

Stage I

Stage II

Stage III

Stage IV

Circle Time

Hall/PE

Literacy

Numeracy

Drama

Small Group

Art

Humanities

Science

Design Technology

PHSE

Food Technology

THINKING & REASONING

Be Polite!

Aim
To be able to distinguish genuine thanks or praise from polite evasions.

Equipment

'Be Polite!' questions and their associated responses from Teaching Resources (page 219).

Preparation

Copy and cut out individual question and response cards. Put them in two piles in order.

Activity

Divide the children into two teams. Give the first child in Team A a 'Question' card, and their opposite number the matching 'Response' card. Team A child reads out their question. Team B child reads out the response. The rest of the group must decide whether the Team B child really liked the object in question, or is just trying to be polite. What makes them think so?

Examples

Question: 'What did you think of the fish pie?'
Response: 'It had a most unusual flavour.'
Question: 'Do you like my new hat?'
Response: 'It's wonderful. That blue really suits you.'
Question: 'We are giving you a bread-board for your wedding present. Would you like that?'
Response: 'Thank you so much. It will be nice to be able to use a different one for each day of the week.'

Tip

This game can be a useful introduction to a discussion about 'white lies' and whether they can ever be acceptable.

WORD PLAY

Stage I

Stage II

Stage III

Stage IV

Circle Time

Hall/PE

Literacy

Numeracy

Drama

Small Group

Art

Humanities

Science

Design Technology

PHSE

Food Technology

WORD PLAY

Warm-Ups for Word Play

Lazy Eights

This is a well-known brain gym exercise that uses both sides of the brain, and is thought to stimulate the links between sounds, letters and words. Hold your left thumb at eye level, about 30cm from your face. Very slowly trace a horizontal figure of eight, keeping your eyes on the thumb all the time. Do this three times, then repeat with the right thumb. Repeat using both thumbs, moving together.

Word Links

This is a simple word-association game. The group sits or stands in a circle. Start the game by saying a word. The person on your left has to say the first word they think of. Continue round the circle until everyone has had a turn.

WORD PLAY

Stage I

Stage II

Stage III

Stage IV

Circle Time

Hall/PE

Literacy

Numeracy

Drama

Small Group

Art

Humanities

Science

Design Technology

PHSE

Food Technology

Plus or Minus Pairs

Aim
To understand the words used for addition and subtraction.

Equipment

The 'Plus or Minus Pairs' template from Teaching Resources (page 220).

Preparation

The template needs to be photocopied on to card, (or even better, laminated) and cut out into individual words or signs.

Activity

This is a game for a group of not more than five children. Shuffle the cards and lay them face down on the table. Each child has a go at turning over two cards at random, as in the game of 'Pairs'. If they think the cards mean the same thing they keep their 'pair'. If not, the cards are returned face down on the table. The child with the most pairs at the end is the winner. Give help with reading as necessary.

Tip

You need to explain at the beginning that in this game a 'pair' does not imply that the cards are identical, but that the meaning is the same.

Examples

'Plus' and 'add'.
'Subtract' and 'minus'.

Stage I

Stage II

Stage III

Stage IV

Circle Time

Hall/PE

Literacy

Numeracy

Drama

Small Group

Art

Humanities

Science

Design Technology

PHSE

Food Technology

WORD PLAY

Always, Sometimes, Usually, Never

Aim
To be able to demonstrate an understanding of the words 'always', 'sometimes', 'usually', 'never'.

Equipment

A bean-bag.
Four large pieces of card.

Preparation

Make a list of situations to which the words in the title could apply (see examples).
Tailor them to the children's age and experience. Write each of the title words on separate large pieces of card.

Activity

Divide the group into two teams. Display the word cards so that everyone can see them, and read them out one at a time. Now read out the first situation, and throw the bean-bag to a member of the first team. They must either point to the appropriate word card, or say the word. If they are correct, that team scores a point. If they are wrong, the question is thrown open to both teams. Once the correct word has been chosen, the bean-bag is thrown to a member of the opposing team, and the next situation is read out. Continue in this way until all the situations have been used.

Examples

'Elephants climb trees.' (Never)
'Teachers drink coffee at break time.' (Usually)
'Christmas Day is the 25th December.' (Always)
'Children go to the cinema.' (Sometimes)
'The sun shines in summer.' (Usually)
'It snows in winter.' (Sometimes)
'Fish live in water'. (Always)

WORD PLAY

Stage I

Stage II

Stage III

Stage IV

Circle Time

Hall/PE

Literacy

Numeracy

Drama

Small Group

Art

Humanities

Science

Design Technology

PHSE

Food Technology

Mend the Word

Aim

To be able to blend phonemes together to make a word.

Equipment

'Vowel Detector' pictures from Teaching Resources (pages 227–228).

Preparation

Copy and cut out enough pictures for each child playing to have four turns.

Activity

This activity is suitable for groups of up to eight children. Explain to them that you are going to say some words, broken down into their various sounds or phonemes, and they have to work out what the words are. Decide which child is to go first. Take a picture from your pack, and say its name phoneme by phoneme – for example, *p-ea-ch* (peach). If the child gets the word right, they get the picture card. The winner is the one with the most pictures.

NB Do not split the sounds in consonant digraphs. The 'ch' in 'peach' should be pronounced as a single sound, not 'c' – 'h'.

Stage I
Stage II
Stage III
Stage IV
Circle Time
Hall/PE
Literacy
Numeracy
Drama
Small Group
Art
Humanities
Science
Design Technology
PHSE
Food Technology

WORD PLAY

What a Muddle!

Aim
To understand that words which sound the same can have different meanings.

Equipment

'What a Muddle!' incomplete sentences and pictures from Teaching Resources (pages 221–222).

Preparation

Copy the pictures and sentences and cut them out to make individual cards.

Activity

This game is best for a group of five or six children. Spread out the pictures in front of the children, and keep the incomplete sentences in your hand. Choose a child, and read out a sentence from your pack. Can they find the picture that finishes the sentence? When they have found it, with or without help, read out the completed sentence.

Examples

'I saw a '…' (The child should pick up the picture of a saw.)
'I see the '…' (The child should pick up the picture of the sea.)

Tip

The first four sentences are easiest, and it is best to start with these.

WORD PLAY

Stage I

Stage II

Stage III

Stage IV

Circle Time

Hall/PE

Literacy

Numeracy

Drama

Small Group

Art

Humanities

Science

Design Technology

PHSE

Food Technology

Peculiar Possessions

Aim
To appreciate strange-sounding or onomatopoeic words.

Equipment

None.

Activity

Tell the children that a very strange person has recently moved in to the house next door to you. This person owns some of the oddest things. You are going to tell them the names of some of them. Can the children think what the things might look like? Collect suggestions.

Examples

A wobbly-widget. A sloopy-slime. A crackle-crumble. A blobby-burble. A grease-gruesome. A tippy-toppy. A creepy-critcher. A sad-baggle. A screeper. A flitter-flap. A grarnch. A glum-bug. An ariaswile. A wipsnitch. A scroogle. A patter-wack.

Stage I

Stage II

Stage III

Stage IV

Circle Time

Hall/PE

Literacy

Numeracy

Drama

Small Group

Art

Humanities

Science

Design Technology

PHSE

Food Technology

WORD PLAY

Alphabet Soup

Aim

To be able to generate words in specific categories, starting with specific sounds.

Equipment

None.

Preparation

You may want to jot down some categories. It is also worth testing out some letters to make sure there are enough items in a particular category which start with that letter!

Activity

The children sit in a circle. Explain to them that you are going to pick a category – for example, food, animals, sports, clothing, vehicles, furniture – and then a sound. They are going to take turns to think of items in that category that start with the target sound. Identify the first category and sound, and produce the first word yourself. The child next to you adds a word, and so on round the circle. Then select a different letter and repeat the process. You may want to keep a record of the words.

Examples

Category: food
Sound: 'b'
Words: beans, burger, breakfast, bread, buns, broccoli, butter, beef, bacon.

Tip

Some letters are obviously easier than others. Make sure that the children are thinking about the *sounds* and not the spellings. Non-words are accepted, but listed separately.

WORD PLAY

Count the Sounds

Aim
To be able to detect the number of different phonemes in short words.

Equipment

'Count the Sounds' template from Teaching Resources (page 223).
Two hoops or large sheets of paper.

Preparation

Make several copies of the template, and cut into individual pictures. Each child should have up to ten pictures. Mark the hoops or sheets of paper with a 2 or a 3.

Activity

Shuffle the pictures, and deal an equal number to each child. Place the hoops or sheets of paper in the middle of the table, or on the floor if space permits. Explain to the children that they are to try to sort their cards according to the number of *sounds* in the word. Some of the words will have two sounds, some three. When you say 'Go!', they must start sorting, putting the cards either in the 'two' hoop or the 'three' hoop. When everyone has finished, check to make sure the cards have been sorted correctly.

Tip

The children will need to have been introduced to the idea of segmenting, and to have had some practice before trying this activity. Some children will need to say the words aloud to be successful, while, at a more advanced stage, some will be able to rehearse the words silently in their heads.

Stage I

Stage II

Stage III

Stage IV

Circle Time

Hall/PE

Literacy

Numeracy

Drama

Small Group

Art

Humanities

Science

Design Technology

PHSE

Food Technology

Stage I

Stage II

Stage III

Stage IV

Circle Time

Hall/PE

Literacy

Numeracy

Drama

Small Group

Art

Humanities

Science

Design Technology

PHSE

Food Technology

WORD PLAY

Roots and Shoots

Aim
To be able to make new words from a root word.

Equipment

List of 'Root' words from Teaching Resources (page 224). Pencils and paper.

Preparation

Photocopy the root words onto card, and cut them out. Put the individual words in a hat or box.

Activity

Divide the group into two teams. Explain that the idea is to think of as many words containing the root word as possible in a given time. Give some examples. The team with the most words wins the round. Choose a scribe for each team. This should be someone confident enough to have a go at writing down the words given by the group, without worrying too much about the spelling. Supply them with pencil and paper. Now take a word out of the hat, read it to the teams and stick it up so they can refer to it. Allow one minute, then call 'Stop!'
Repeat with the next word, and so on. This game can last for as long as you want it to, or until the words run out.

Example

Stream: streamer, streamline, slipstream, streaming.

WORD PLAY

Stage I

Stage II

Stage III

Stage IV

Circle Time

Hall/PE

Literacy

Numeracy

Drama

Small Group

Art

Humanities

Science

Design Technology

PHSE

Food Technology

Gridlock (1)

Aim
To understand a range of synonyms.

Equipment

'Gridlock (1)' list of synonyms and grid form from Teaching Resources (pages 225–226).

Preparation

Copy a grid and list of synonyms for each team or group playing.

Activity

Divide the children into groups or teams. Give each group a grid form, and a list which consists of one 'starter' word and a range of synonyms. A few 'distractor' words are also included. Explain to the children that they have to fill in their grids by writing in each square a word which means much the same as the 'starter' word. Some of the words are there to trick them. The teams should elect one person to act as scribe and write in the words. They need to understand that they must discuss and reach consensus about which words to include. When all the teams have finished, one child from each group reads out their 'starter' word and the synonyms they have chosen. Do the rest of the children agree? Can they think of any more?

Tip

Starter word: big
Synonyms: huge, vast, enormous, colossal, massive, gigantic
Distractors: wonderful, strong, alarming, wild, brilliant

Examples

Other good starter words: quick, slow, happy, sad, clever, stupid.
Some words will turn up quite appropriately in different grids. If the level of vocabulary is too advanced for the group, block out some of the squares on the grid and remove some of the harder synonyms.

Stage I

Stage II

Stage III

Stage IV

Circle Time

Hall/PE

Literacy

Numeracy

Drama

Small Group

Art

Humanities

Science

Design Technology

PHSE

Food Technology

WORD PLAY

Vowel Detector (1)

Aim

To be able to recognise the short vowel in single syllable words.

Equipment

'Vowel Detector (1)' pictures of single-syllable words containing short vowels 'a', 'e', 'i', 'o', 'u' as in 'hat', 'bed', 'pig', 'top', 'bus' from Teaching Resources (pages 227–228).
Paper.

Preparation

Write the short vowels on separate sheets of paper and put them in different places around the room. Copy the pictures and cut them out to make individual cards.

Activity

This is a game for six to eight children, standing or seated round a table. The pictures are placed face down in a pile. The first child takes the top picture and says what it is. They then have to work out which vowel sound it contains, and go to stand by the appropriate letter, taking their picture with them. When everybody is standing by their vowel sign, choose the most confident reader in each group to collect the pictures and say all their names. If time permits, and there are enough pictures left, play another round.

WORD PLAY

| Stage I |
| Stage II |
| Stage III |
| Stage IV |
| Circle Time |
| Hall/PE |
| Literacy |
| Numeracy |
| Drama |
| Small Group |
| Art |
| Humanities |
| Science |
| Design Technology |
| PHSE |
| Food Technology |

Take Your Partners

Aim
To become familiar with the way in which words can be combined to form compound words.

Equipment

List of words (see examples below).

Preparation

Make a slip of paper or card with half a compound word on it for every child playing.

Activity

Give every child a word, making sure that for every one you give out, someone has its pair. Make sure that everyone can read their word. Tell the children that when you say 'Go!', they are to hunt for their 'word partners', and then stand still together until everybody has their pair. Ask each pair what their compound word is.

Examples

foot+ball, hair+dresser, battle+ship, pig+sty, farm+yard, hay+stack, letter+box, dust+bin, door+step, eye+lash, bumble+bee, light+house, coat+hook, foot+path, bath+mat.

Extension

Ask the children if they can think of any more compound words. They could use words from the above examples in different ways – for example, coat+hanger, money+box, day+time, door+knocker, eye+brow, battle+field – or think of new ones.

You might make this into a race, the winner being the first pair to team up.

Stage I
Stage II
Stage III
Stage IV
Circle Time
Hall/PE
Literacy
Numeracy
Drama
Small Group
Art
Humanities
Science
Design Technology
PHSE
Food Technology

WORD PLAY

Find the Phonemes

Aim
To be able to say the individual phonemes in a word – sound segmenting.

Equipment

'Vowel Detector' pictures from Teaching Resources (pages 227–228).

Preparation

Copy and cut out a good selection of the pictures. When you first play this game, choose only cv, vc or cvc words (for example 's-ea','ar-m', 'b- a –t'). Leave the ones with consonant blends until the children have had some practice at this level. You may want to link this activity with spelling patterns the children are learning.

Activity

This is a game for a small group. It is similar to 'Count the Sounds', except that this time the children have not only to distinguish, but also to remember and say, all the separate phonemes in the word. Shuffle the cards and deal three or four cards to each player. Put the rest of the pack face down in the middle. The children can hold their cards in a fan and choose which one they want to segment. Take turns around the circle. If the children segment the words into the correct phonemes, they put the card on the bottom of the central pack. If not, they must keep that card and take another from the pack. The winner is the first to get rid of all their cards.

WORD PLAY

Gridlock (2)

Aim
To understand a range of antonyms (opposites).

Equipment

'Gridlock (2)' list of antonyms (page 229) and grid form from 'Gridlock (1)' (page 225) from Teaching Resources.

Preparation

Copy a grid and a list of antonyms for each team or group playing.

Activity

This game is played exactly like 'Gridlock (1)' but this time the children are looking for words of opposite meaning to the starter word.

Examples

Starter word: gentle
Antonyms: rough, cruel, unkind, harsh, fierce, violent, hard, brutal
Distractors: busy, rapid, hardworking

Tips

Some words will turn up quite appropriately in different grids. If the level of vocabulary is too advanced for the group, block out some of the squares on the grid and remove some of the harder words.

Stage I

Stage II

Stage III

Stage IV

Circle Time

Hall/PE

Literacy

Numeracy

Drama

Small Group

Art

Humanities

Science

Design Technology

PHSE

Food Technology

Stage I

Stage II

Stage III

Stage IV

Circle Time

Hall/PE

Literacy

Numeracy

Drama

Small Group

Art

Humanities

Science

Design Technology

PHSE

Food Technology

WORD PLAY

Vowel Detector (2)

Aim
To be able to identify long vowel sounds – 'ee', 'oo', 'ah', 'aw', 'er'.

Equipment

'Vowel Detector (2)' word list and pictures from Teaching Resources (pages 230–231).
Paper.

Preparation

Write the long vowel sounds on separate pieces of paper. As there are several different ways of writing the long vowel phonemes, we have chosen the spelling choice that matches the pictures. Copy the pictures, and cut them into individual cards or slips.

Activity

This is played in the same way as 'Vowel Detector (1)'. The vowel cards are placed in different parts of the room. The picture cards are laid face down in a pile. Each child takes a picture from the pile, and goes to the vowel card they think is correct. When everybody is standing by the right vowel card, choose one child from each group to call out the names of all their pictures.

WORD PLAY

	Stage I
	Stage II
	Stage III
	Stage IV
	Circle Time
	Hall/PE
	Literacy
	Numeracy
	Drama
	Small Group
	Art
	Humanities
	Science
	Design Technology
	PHSE
	Food Technology

What's it Like?

Aim

To understand the use of similes.

Equipment

List of incomplete phrases.
List of similes.

Preparation

Copy the incomplete phrases on to individual slips or cards, a full set for each pair playing. Copy a list of similes for each pair.

Activity

Divide the children into pairs, seated at tables. Give each pair a container, into which you have put the collection of incomplete phrases. You also give them the list of similes. Tell the children they have two minutes in which to draw out the phrases, one by one, taking turns. They then help each other find the appropriate simile, and when they have reached agreement, one of the partners writes it on the phrase card. Then give them another minute or so to see if they can think of one or more additional simile for each phrase, and write them in. Some are much easier than others, so it is no disgrace if they cannot think of one! The pairs then share the results with the whole group.

Example

Black as: night (pitch, the ace of spades, ink)
White as: snow (a lily, a sheet, a ghost)
Run like: the wind (a stag)

Tips

It is a good idea to go through one example with the children before they start.

Stage I

Stage II

Stage III

Stage IV

Circle Time

Hall/PE

Literacy

Numeracy

Drama

Small Group

Art

Humanities

Science

Design Technology

PHSE

Food Technology

WORD PLAY

Sounds and Stopwatch

Aim
To be able to think of alliterative words by word category.

Equipment

Two dice made from small wooden bricks, with one of the following phonemes written on each face – p, b, m, t, d, s, f, g, c, sh, l, w.
A stopwatch.

Activity

Divide the children into teams of three. Each team appoints a captain. Explain that you will throw a die, and the competing team must produce a sentence in which the three important words start with the sound shown on the die. Each member of the teams is allocated a word category – subject, verb, or object. Select a team to start. Roll one of the dice, and start the stopwatch.
Suppose the die falls on 'p'. The 'subject' team member must produce a noun beginning with 'p' – for example, 'puppy'. The second team member (responsible for the 'verb') might say 'picks', and the third team member (responsible for the 'object') might say 'paper'. The team captain then puts the sentence together, and says, 'The puppy picks up the paper.' There is a time limit of one minute.

Tip

You need to remind the children that they are thinking about sounds not spelling. Therefore, the 'c' sound (as in 'cat') is the same as the 'k' sound (as in 'kitten'); and the 's' and 'sh' sounds are two distinct phonemes.
You might want to practise producing lists of alliterative nouns and verbs as a preliminary to this game.

WORD PLAY

Stage I

Stage II

Stage III

Stage IV

Circle Time

Hall/PE

Literacy

Numeracy

Drama

Small Group

Art

Humanities

Science

Design Technology

PHSE

Food Technology

This Way and That

Aim
To be able to use a range of adverbs to enhance meaning and interest.

Equipment

Lists of verbs and adverbs from Teaching Resources (page 232).

Preparation

Copy the lists of verbs and adverbs and cut them into individual slips. You will need enough verb slips for each child to have one, and lots of complete sets of all the adverb slips.

Activity

Seat the children in threes or fours around their tables. Give each child a different verb slip, and scatter one of the adverb sets on the table in the middle. Explain that when you say 'Go!', they have to hunt through the adverbs and collect any that they think could be paired with their verb. Some adverbs will be appropriate for more than one verb. After about two minutes, ask the children to read out their verb and the adverbs they have gathered to go with it, in turn. Are there any objections? Can they justify their choice?

Example

Verb: run
Adverbs: quickly, silently, nastily, greedily, rapidly, slowly, unkindly, fairly

Stage I

Stage II

Stage III

Stage IV

Circle Time

Hall/PE

Literacy

Numeracy

Drama

Small Group

Art

Humanities

Science

Design Technology

PHSE

Food Technology

WORD PLAY

Call My Bluff

Aim
To enjoy the sound of strange words, and discover the meaning of some of them.

Equipment

'Call My Bluff' list of words from Teaching Resources (page 233).

Preparation

Have the word list ready for use. Words in bold are nonsense words.

Activity

Divide the children into teams or groups. Explain that you are going to read out lots of strange-sounding words. Some of them will be real words, and some will be made up. They must try to guess which is which. Keep a note of points awarded for correct guesses, and explain the meanings of the real words as you go along.

Example

Borborygmus (tummy rumbling)
Bandersnatch

Extension

Read the children some of the poems or prose from which invented words may have been taken, principally the works of Lewis Carroll and Edward Lear.
Challenge the children to produce some written work using a few of the real words.

WORD PLAY

Stage I

Stage II

Stage III

Stage IV

Circle Time

Hall/PE

Literacy

Numeracy

Drama

Small Group

Art

Humanities

Science

Design Technology

PHSE

Food Technology

What's Cooking?

Aim
To be able to link the initial sound of a word with a narrow category.

Equipment

Pictures of different foods cut from magazines.
Two dice made from wooden bricks.

Preparation

Label each face of one die with a food category – for example, fruit, vegetables, dairy, meat, cereal, fish. Label each face of the second die with a letter of the alphabet.

Activity

This game is suitable for a group of up to eight children. They take turns to roll both dice, and have to try to think of an item in the target category that begins with the target letter. For instance if they throw a 'p', and the category die lands on 'vegetables', they might think of 'potato' or 'pumpkin'.

Tip

This activity links with the Year 3 Science topic on Healthy Eating.
You can make the game more challenging for abler or older pupils by using categories such as 'carbohydrates' and 'fats'.

Stage I

Stage II

Stage III

Stage IV

Circle Time

Hall/PE

Literacy

Numeracy

Drama

Small Group

Art

Humanities

Science

Design Technology

PHSE

Food Technology

WORD PLAY

Vowel Detector (3)

Aim
To be able to recognise the vowel diphthongs 'oa' (as in' boat') , 'ay' (as in 'day'), 'eye' (as in 'pie'), 'oi' (as in 'coin') and 'ow' (as in 'cow').

Equipment

'Vowel Detector (3)' word list and pictures from Teaching Resources (pages 234–235).

Preparation

Write the vowel diphthongs on separate pieces of paper. As there are several different ways of writing vowel diphthongs, we have chosen the spelling choice that matches most of the pictures. Copy the pictures and cut them out to make individual cards or slips.

Activity

This game is played in the same way as 'Vowel Detector' (1) and (2). The vowel cards are placed in different parts of the room. The picture cards are laid face down in a pile. Each child takes a picture from the pile, and goes to the vowel card they think is correct. When everybody is standing by the right vowel card, choose one child from each group to call out the names of all their pictures.

WORD PLAY

Stage I

Stage II

Stage III

Stage IV

Circle Time

Hall/PE

Literacy

Numeracy

Drama

Small Group

Art

Humanities

Science

Design Technology

PHSE

Food Technology

My Granny Said

Aim

To understand the meaning of some proverbs.

Equipment

List of 'My Granny Said' proverbs from Teaching Resources (page 236).

Preparation

Copy the list of proverbs and cut it up to make separate slips.

Activity

Divide the children into pairs or small groups. Give each pair or group a proverb slip. Explain that they have two minutes in which to try to work out what the proverb means. At the end of the time, ask the pairs or groups in turn to read out their proverb, and give their explanation. Encourage discussion as to whether the meaning is right or wrong, and if wrong, what the correct meaning might be. Provide the answer if need be. Then move on to the next pair or group.

Examples

A stitch in time saves nine. Take care of the pennies and the pounds will take care of themselves. The early bird catches the worm.

WORD PLAY

Stage I

Stage II

Stage III

Stage IV

Circle Time

Hall/PE

Literacy

Numeracy

Drama

Small Group

Art

Humanities

Science

Design Technology

PHSE

Food Technology

Fix It!

Aim
To become familiar with the way in which some prefixes and suffixes are used.

Equipment

Lists of prefixes and suffixes, and words to which they can be attached from Teaching Resources (page 237).

Preparation

Copy and cut out a prefix or suffix for each Head of Family, and the appropriate words to go with them, on individual slips.

Activity

Choose two or three children to be Heads of the Families. Give each Head a slip or card with a prefix or suffix on it. Distribute the corresponding words on slips of paper or cards to the rest of the children. (You can adjust the number of Heads and the number of words you give out according to the number of children taking part – each prefix or suffix has a minimum of eight corresponding words.) Explain to the children that the family Heads are to go round the group finding out what word each child has. When the Head thinks his prefix or suffix goes with that word, he 'collects' that child as part of his family. When all the children have been allocated to a family, it is time to check for correctness, and to explain the meaning of any words that are unfamiliar. Some children could belong in more than one family, so arbitration may be needed!

Example

Prefix: Mis
Words: fortune, take, leading, understand, place, fit, trust, behave, conduct, direct, count.

Extension

Include words whose stem has to change – for example, 'pity' – 'pitiless'. Add further prefixes – for example, 'in' and suffixes – for example, 'ship', 'hood'.

WORD PLAY

Stage I

Stage II

Stage III

Stage IV

Circle Time

Hall/PE

Literacy

Numeracy

Drama

Small Group

Art

Humanities

Science

Design Technology

PHSE

Food Technology

Gridlock (3)

Aim
To be able to distinguish between words which sound the same but have different meanings.

Equipment

'Gridlock (3)' grids and word lists from Teaching Resources (pages 238–239).

Preparation

Copy and enlarge the grids, and copy the word lists. You may like to cut out the words into separate 'tiles'.

Activity

This is a game for a maximum of 12 players. Divide the children into two or three groups of three or four. Give each group a grid, and its corresponding words, either cut out into tiles or as shown. The children either place the tiles in the appropriate space on the grid, or write the words in. The first group to achieve a correctly completed grid is the winner. When all groups have finished, the children take turns to read the sentences aloud.

Example

The knight fought bravely, but as night fell it grew too dark to see.

Tips

For children who cannot quite manage this activity, fill in the words in the first half of the sentence for them.

Extension

Give the children blank grids, so that they have to find the paired words and make up their own sentences.

Stage I

Stage II

Stage III

Stage IV

Circle Time

Hall/PE

Literacy

Numeracy

Drama

Small Group

Art

Humanities

Science

Design Technology

PHSE

Food Technology

WORD PLAY

Author!

Aim
To know some 'powerful' verbs and have an idea how to use them.

Equipment

Short paragraphs and lists of powerful verbs from Teaching Resources (page 241).

Preparation

Copy and cut out paragraphs and lists of alternative verbs.

Activity

This activity can be carried out either by the children individually, or in small groups. Small groups are preferable, as they provide an opportunity for discussion and debate. Give each group one of the short paragraphs, and the list of powerful verbs. They must decide among themselves which powerful verbs to insert instead of the existing verbs, and write them in. When everybody has finished, a spokesman for each group reads out their paragraph, giving it full dramatic value!

Example

The tiger seemed to be asleep.
The keeper (walked)… as quietly as he could towards the sleeping animal.
(ambled, crept, pottered, sauntered, strode)
As he approached, to his horror the tiger suddenly (got up)…
(jumped up, leapt up, reared up)

EXPLAINING
≠ DESCRIBING

Stage I

Stage II

Stage III

Stage IV

Circle Time

Hall/PE

Literacy

Numeracy

Drama

Small
Group

Art

Humanities

Science

Design
Technology

PHSE

Food
Technology

EXPLAINING & DESCRIBING

Warm Ups for Explaining and Describing

Balance

Stand with feet about a shoulders' width apart, with your arms at your sides. Slowly shift your weight onto your right foot. At the same time raise the left knee to just below waist height. Hold this position for a few seconds. Then clasp the knee with both hands and continue to hold for a few seconds longer. Slowly unclasp your hands, and lower your foot to a standing position. Repeat the action with the right knee. Regular practice will improve balance, and you will be able to hold the position for longer. Focusing your gaze on a fixed point will help you to maintain your balance.

What's for Tea?

The aim of this activity is to communicate without speaking or writing. Explain to the group that they will be trying to answer a question without speaking or writing. You will need a supply of answers, written on slips of paper – see examples below. Tell them that the question is 'What's for tea?' Choose someone from the group to start. If necessary help them read the first answer. They then have to try to convey it to the rest of the group. Anyone who thinks they know what it is puts their hand up. The child with the first correct answer takes the next turn.

Examples

Chicken and chips	A cup of tea
A bowl of cereal	Spaghetti Bolognese
Pizza	A packet of crisps
Ice cream	Two bananas
A boiled egg	A Chinese Takeaway

EXPLAINING & DESCRIBING

Keep it Going

Aim
To be able to define an object by category, use, attributes, properties, location and similarities.

Equipment

None.

Activity

Seat the children in a circle. Explain that you are going to name an object. In turn round the circle, the children are to say something about that object. The list keeps going until nobody can think of anything else to add, at which point you introduce a new object.
Challenge the children to keep going up to eight or more ideas at a time.

Example

Apple: It's a fruit; you can eat it; it grows on trees; it's round; may be red or green; it has a peel; you can make it into apple pies; it has pips; you can buy it in the supermarket or greengrocer's.
Horse: It's an animal; it has four legs; it has a mane and tail; it can be black, brown, grey or dappled; you can ride on it; it can run fast; it can jump; it can pull carts; it can run in races; it can bite and kick; it may live on a farm; it's a bit like a donkey.

Tips

You may need to do a trial run first, so that the children understand the range of ideas they can contribute. If they run out of ideas too quickly, prompt by asking: 'What sort of a thing is it?' (category) 'What can you do with it?' (use), and so on.

Stage I

Stage II

Stage III

Stage IV

Circle Time

Hall/PE

Literacy

Numeracy

Drama

Small Group

Art

Humanities

Science

Design Technology

PHSE

Food Technology

EXPLAINING & DESCRIBING

Stage I

Stage II

Stage III

Stage IV

Circle Time

Hall/PE

Literacy

Numeracy

Drama

Small Group

Art

Humanities

Science

Design Technology

PHSE

Food Technology

Adjective Ladder

Aim
To be able to use specific descriptive vocabulary in a sentence.

Equipment

'Adjective Ladder' templates from Teaching Resources (pages 242–244).
A supply of counters.

Preparation

Photocopy a ladder and the words, for each team playing, onto card if possible. Cut them all out. Divide the word cards into easy and difficult adjectives. Put a green spot on the back of the easy cards, and a red spot on the back of the harder cards.

Activity

Divide the children into teams, each of which has its ladder picture. Place the cards in three piles (pictures, easy adjectives and difficult adjectives). A child from each team takes turns to pick a picture card and either an easy green word card or a difficult red word card. The child has to say a sentence using both the cards chosen. If they produce an acceptable sentence, they move the counter up their ladder. Score as follows: move up one rung for a green card and two rungs for a red card. The winning team is the first to reach the top of the ladder.

Example

The child picks up a picture of a rabbit, and the word 'old'. He says the sentence: 'An old rabbit was sitting in the field.'

Extension

Additional sets of cards can be made, using a wider vocabulary and harder adjectives.

EXPLAINING & DESCRIBING

Stage I

Stage II

Stage III

Stage IV

Circle Time

Hall/PE

Literacy

Numeracy

Drama

Small Group

Art

Humanities

Science

Design Technology

PHSE

Food Technology

Jumpers

Aim

To be able to use descriptions involving colour, number, shape and pattern.

Equipment

A simple outline drawing of a jumper.
Paper and crayons.

Activity

Give each child a piece of paper and access to crayons. Show the children the outline of the jumper, and tell them to copy it on to their paper. Give help if necessary. Now tell the children to colour their jumpers, using any pattern they may choose. You may feel it necessary to have a preliminary discussion about spots, stripes and other shapes, and to revise vocabulary such as 'straight' and 'wiggly'. Tell the children they are not to put their names on their pictures. When they have finished, collect the pictures and spread them out on a table. Put in two or three extra jumpers that you have coloured. Each child then tries to describe his picture, until you and the other children are able to identify it. Question and prompt as necessary, but make sure the child does not point! When the jumper has been correctly identified, its owner can pick it up and keep it.

Example

A blue jumper with two yellow stars in the middle.
A jumper with green and white stripes.

Extension

Play again, encouraging the children to produce ever more imaginative and complicated designs. This is a good way of extending descriptive vocabulary.

Stage I

Stage II

Stage III

Stage IV

Circle Time

Hall/PE

Literacy

Numeracy

Drama

Small Group

Art

Humanities

Science

Design Technology

PHSE

Food Technology

EXPLAINING & DESCRIBING

Martian Mysteries

Aim
To be able to explain the function of everyday items.

Equipment

None.

Activity

Explain to the children that they are all Martians. They have arrived on earth and keep coming across things that are a mystery to them. Choose one child at a time, and whisper to them the name of an object. They have to tell the group of Martians what the object is used for, and see how quickly they can guess what it is. If they cannot guess immediately, questioning is in order. This may need to be led by the adult at first. As soon as the item is guessed, the 'explainer' is given a clap.

Example

a mobile phone
a television
a fridge
a washing machine
an iron
a motor mower
an electric torch
roller blades
a skateboard
a pair of skis

Tip

Young children often tend to give the game away by naming the object. You may need to emphasise several times, 'Don't say what it is – say what you do with it'.

Extension

Choose more complicated items – for example, a steam roller, a computer, a helicopter, a calculator, a calendar.

EXPLAINING & DESCRIBING

Stage I

Stage II

Stage III

Stage IV

Circle Time

Hall/PE

Literacy

Numeracy

Drama

Small Group

Art

Humanities

Science

Design Technology

PHSE

Food Technology

Sentence Anagrams

Aim

To be able to assemble a sentence from individual words.

Equipment

Simple sentences, using familiar vocabulary.

Preparation

Make two copies of each sentence. Cut them into individual words. The teams will be divided into pairs, each of which has a sentence.(A team of six children will therefore need three sentences.)

Activity

Divide the children into two teams. The first two children in each team are given the same sets of words which, when put together correctly, will form a simple sentence. It is easier to manage this activity if there is an adult for each team. Lay out the words in random order, the right way up, and give help with reading if necessary. When you say 'Go!', the pairs from each team race to assemble their sentence. As soon as they have finished, they pick up their words and come and whisper their sentence to the adult. Then the next pair are given their words and take a turn. The first team to finish wins.

Example

The postman drives a red van.

Tips

You can tailor the length and complexity of the sentences to the children's ability. Sentences can be linked to Literacy Hour or topic work if appropriate.

EXPLAINING & DESCRIBING

Stage I

Stage II

Stage III

Stage IV

Circle Time

Hall/PE

Literacy

Numeracy

Drama

Small Group

Art

Humanities

Science

Design Technology

PHSE

Food Technology

Character Building

Aim
To be able to describe an imaginary character or creature.

Equipment

None.

Activity

Tell the children that they are going to help describe some imaginary people and creatures. Start them off with a brief scenario, and then take suggestions from each child in the group, in turn.

Example

Adult says: 'I'm thinking of a very special and unusual bird, which has escaped from the zoo.' Choose a child to start the description off – 'How big do you think it is?' and prompt further, as necessary, when you move on to the next child – for example, 'What colour?' 'What size wings?' 'What shape beak?'
Other examples might be: 'I'm thinking of an alien who has just stepped out of a space ship.' 'I'm thinking of the captain in charge of a pirate ship.' 'I'm thinking of a goblin who lives under a tree root.'

Tips

Some discussion and mild argument should be allowed. When the game has been played once or twice, the children should not need suggestions from you before producing ideas.

Extension

At the end you might get one child to give the complete description. The children could try drawing the character they have described.

EXPLAINING & DESCRIBING

Stage I

Stage II

Stage III

Stage IV

Circle Time

Hall/PE

Literacy

Numeracy

Drama

Small Group

Art

Humanities

Science

Design Technology

PHSE

Food Technology

Senior Snap

Aim

To be able to explain the different ways in which two pictures may have something in common.

Equipment

Any collection of coloured pictures taken from a variety of sources – they must not all be from the same category, such as all animals or all plants. The pictures should be of single items.

Activity

Seat the children so that all of them can see you. Explain that you are going to hold up two pictures at a time. Anyone who thinks they can identify a way in which the two pictures have something in common must put their hand up. Select a child to explain their idea. If the explanation is wrong, or insufficiently clear, another child has a go. Then discard one of the pictures and choose another to pair it with. Continue until all the pictures are used up. This can be played as a team game, with correct ideas and explanations earning points.

Examples

Pictures can by linked by attributes, category, season, shape, use, where found, and so on. For example a red flower, and a post van: are both red. A snowball and a woolly jumper: snow falls in the winter, and you wear warm jumpers in the winter. A paper boat and a kite: both are toys.

Tip

It may be necessary to have one or two demonstrations at the beginning, to show some of the many ways in which two pictures can have something in common.

EXPLAINING & DESCRIBING

Stage I

Stage II

Stage III

Stage IV

Circle Time

Hall/PE

Literacy

Numeracy

Drama

Small Group

Art

Humanities

Science

Design Technology

PHSE

Food Technology

Sentence Jumble

Aim
To be able to re-assemble a muddled up sentence.

Equipment

Sentence cards.

Preparation

Prepare some sentence cards. Each sentence needs to have a subject, an action and a place. Cut the sentences up as shown, and sort into 'subject', 'action' and 'place' piles, labelled 'A', 'B' and 'C'. Each pile of cards is now shuffled, so that cards will be drawn in random order.

Activity

Divide the children into three groups, 'A', 'B' and 'C'. A child from each group takes a card from the corresponding pile. The team of three then have to try to make a sentence using all three cards. When they have finished, one of them reads out the sentence, and the rest of the children decide whether it goes into an 'silly' pile or a 'sensible' pile. Give help with the reading as necessary.

Example

A	B	C
The pig	had a bath	up a tree.
My best friend	lived	in a dustbin.

EXPLAINING & DESCRIBING

Stage I
Stage II
Stage III
Stage IV
Circle Time
Hall/PE
Literacy
Numeracy
Drama
Small Group
Art
Humanities
Science
Design Technology
PHSE
Food Technology

Ifs and Buts

Aim

To be able to use 'if', 'but', 'so' and 'when' in a sentence.

Equipment

The Raceboard from Teaching Resources (page 198). Incomplete sentences and IF, BUT, SO and WHEN cards from Teaching Resources (pages 245–246).
A coloured counter or token for each player, and a die.

Preparation

Copy and cut out a deck of IF, BUT, SO and WHEN cards, and a deck of incomplete sentences.

Activity

This is a game for a small group. Choose one child to go first. They roll the die, and move the number of squares indicated on the raceboard. If they land on a starred square, they pick up an IF, BUT, SO or WHEN card, while you pick up an incomplete sentence card and read it out to them. They must try to finish the sentence using the word in their hand. A plausible and correct sentence earns a point. If a player lands on a smiley face, they go forward one space, if on a sad face, back one space.

Example

I like going on the train... if I can have a corner seat.
but I do get bored.
so I can look out of the window.
when I go to visit my Grandma.

Stage I

Stage II

Stage III

Stage IV

Circle Time

Hall/PE

Literacy

Numeracy

Drama

Small Group

Art

Humanities

Science

Design Technology

PHSE

Food Technology

EXPLAINING & DESCRIBING

Heads, Bodies and Tails

Aim
To be able to generate a detailed description of a person or creature.

Equipment

Blackboard, whiteboard, or flipchart.

Activity

You may want to confine this activity to a maximum of about 15 or 16 children. Divide the children into three groups. Explain that each group has to decide what person or creature they want to create. Give them time to discuss this, out of earshot of each other. Then send two groups out of the room. The remaining group gives you a careful description of the head of the person or creature they have decided on, and you draw it to their instruction on the board or flipchart. You then cover it up with a sheet of flipchart paper, leaving just the neck showing. The first group goes out of the room, and the second group comes in. They describe the body of their person or creature, and you attach it to the existing neck. Repeat with the third group, who describe to you the legs or tail that they have decided on. Then re-convene the whole group, and unveil the composite creature they have invented.

Extension

Try having one child describe the completed picture to the rest of the group, who are not shown it. Can they draw it to his or her instructions? Ask for names for the creature the children have invented.

EXPLAINING & DESCRIBING

	Stage I
	Stage II
	Stage III
	Stage IV
	Circle Time
	Hall/PE
	Literacy
	Numeracy
	Drama
	Small Group
	Art
	Humanities
	Science
	Design Technology
	PHSE
	Food Technology

Spaghetti

Aim

To be able to explain quickly why some objects are unsuitable for particular tasks.

Equipment

A stopwatch.

Preparation

Jot down some ideas for questions.

Activity

This game can be played by individual children seated in a circle, or by teams, with team members being questioned alternately. The emphasis is on obtaining quick responses, so special arrangements will have to be made for any child who is likely to find it difficult. (The solution might be to put the children in pairs, allowing either one of each pair to provide the answer.) Tell the children you are going to fire questions at them, and they will have four seconds in which to reply. If four seconds elapse without the child providing an answer, move straight on to the next child, and save the unanswered question for someone else.

Examples

Why can't we stir a cup of tea with spaghetti?
Why can't we dig the garden with a stick of liquorice?
Why can't we hang the washing out on a line made of wool?
Why don't we make chairs out of cardboard?
Why don't they make clothes out of glass?
Why don't boats have drain holes in the bottom?
Why can't we undo a screw with a wooden spoon?
Why can't we hammer a nail in with a stick of candyfloss?
Why don't we eat soup with our fingers?
Why can't we fill up the car with water instead of petrol?

Stage I

Stage II

Stage III

Stage IV

Circle Time

Hall/PE

Literacy

Numeracy

Drama

Small Group

Art

Humanities

Science

Design Technology

PHSE

Food Technology

EXPLAINING & DESCRIBING

Why Oh Why?

Aim
To be able to explain the reason for generally accepted routine activities.

Equipment

None.

Preparation

Jot down a list of everyday activities. Have these ready to prime the questioners.

Activity

Divide the children into two teams. In turns, a child in Team A asks a child in Team B why we should carry out a particular routine activity. After some group discussion, a child in Team B gives a justification. The adult must adjudicate. If the explanation is felt to be valid, Team B gains a point. Then the teams swap over, with Team B asking for reasons why we should carry out another routine activity. The first team to achieve a certain number of points is the winner.

Example

Questions could include: Why should we clean our teeth twice a day? Why should we learn to read? Why should we cross roads on zebra crossings? Why should drivers obey speed limits? Why should we wash our hair? Why should we have to pass a test before we are allowed to drive a car? (Unsatisfactory reasons include: 'Because my Mum says so', and 'Because you'll go to prison if you don't.')

Tip

It is really important to get the children to think of reasons that convince them of the importance of these activities, rather than politically correct responses.

EXPLAINING & DESCRIBING

Stage I

Stage II

Stage III

Stage IV

Circle Time

Hall/PE

Literacy

Numeracy

Drama

Small Group

Art

Music

Science

Design Technology

PHSE

Food Technology

Tell Me How

Aim

To be able to describe how certain tools and instruments are used.

Equipment

A collection of musical instruments and/or other pieces of equipment.

Activity

Choose one child to be the instructor and one child to carry out the instructions. The instructor must say, step by step, how a particular instrument is held and played, or how the piece of equipment is used. He must not gesture! The second child has the instrument or piece of equipment, and follows the instructions one at a time, *exactly* as they are given. When something goes wrong, the 'audience' must call out 'Stop!' The instructor must then try to correct the mistake and change the instructions until the actions are correct. Then choose another pair of children, and another instrument, and repeat the activity.

Example

The performer has a violin. The instructor must explain how the instrument is held; how the bow is held; how it is placed on the strings; how it is drawn across the strings; and how the other hand 'stops' the strings to change the notes.

Tips

It is probably a good idea for an adult to take the part of the performer for the first go at this activity. You need to demonstrate that you are following the instructions, not just carrying out the actions that you know to be right. Some objects are much easier than others – for example, a drum is easy.

Stage I

Stage II

Stage III

Stage IV

Circle Time

Hall/PE

Literacy

Numeracy

Drama

Small Group

Art

Humanities

Science

Design Technology

PHSE

Food Technology

EXPLAINING & DESCRIBING

Instamatic

Aim
To be able to look carefully at the room, and describe it accurately and in some detail from memory.

Equipment

A blindfold or mask.
Paper and pencils.

Activity

This is an activity to try in different locations at various times, as only two can have a turn at one session. Choose a child to go first. Explain that they will have a minute to look round the room carefully before being blindfolded. They must then describe the room, with as much detail as they can include. Encourage them to start by mentioning the shape and size of the room, before embarking on detail. They have two minutes in which to give as much information as possible. The rest of the group can jot down any factual errors (wrong number of doors or windows, forgetting the television, whiteboard to the left of the door instead of the right, and so on). When the two minutes are up, the group reports on the mistakes made. Then a second child has a go. You could play this again on another occasion, and/or in a different room or outside.

EXPLAINING & DESCRIBING

Stage I

Stage II

Stage III

Stage IV

Circle Time

Hall/PE

Literacy

Numeracy

Drama

Small Group

Art

Humanities

Science

Design Technology

PHSE

Food Technology

Look No Hands!

Aim
To be able to describe three-dimensional shapes, without using gesture.

Equipment

A collection of three-dimensional shapes taken from the appropriate numeracy level.

Preparation

You will need at least as many objects as there are children playing.

Activity

This game is for a group of six or eight children. Divide the children into two teams. Explain that a child from one team is going to try to describe one of the shapes, without using their hands to gesture or point, and without naming the shape. The children in the other team keep guessing, and the 'describer' keeps trying to make things clearer, until the shape is correctly identified. Then give someone from the second team a go.

Tip

You might like to introduce this game by asking the children to describe a spiral staircase. It is likely that they will all use a round and round and upwards gesture with one or both hands. Tell them that they are going to have to do their describing without using their hands.

EXPLAINING & DESCRIBING

Stage I
Stage II
Stage III
Stage IV
Circle Time
Hall/PE
Literacy
Numeracy
Drama
Small Group
Art
Humanities
Science
Design Technology
PHSE
Food Technology

Dictionary

Aim
To be able to define a noun quickly and comprehensively.

Equipment

None.

Preparation

Jot down a list of the examples below, adding any more you can think of. They must require quite sophisticated definitions.

Activity

Divide the children into two or more teams. You will need enough nouns on your list for all the children playing. Explain that your publishing company is compiling a dictionary, and you need good definitions for a lot of words which are not always easy to explain. You will ask members of each team in turn for a definition. They must keep a score of which ones you say your publishers will accept, and which ones they will not. At the end the teams count up their scores. The team with the highest number of accepted definitions is the winner.

Examples

a choir	an orchestra
an aquarium	an aviary
a zoo	an army
a game reserve	a safari
an election	a debate
a parade	a flower show
a funfair	the Olympics
a football match	a parliament
a department store	a supermarket
a village fête	

EXPLAINING & DESCRIBING

Stage I

Stage II

Stage III

Stage IV

Circle Time

Hall/PE

Literacy

Numeracy

Drama

Small Group

Art

Humanities

Science

Design Technology

PHSE

Food Technology

Trailblazers

Aim
To be able to think of suitable signs to accompany a text, and to explain what they look like.

Equipment

'Trailblazers' short texts from Teaching Resources (pages 247–248).
Coloured pencils and paper for the children.

Preparation

Select two or three texts to read.

Activity

Explain to the children that you are going to read them short paragraphs about some journeys. Whenever you pause, they are to draw a sign that will help the travellers identify – for example, the direction to take, a possible danger, or a good place to stop and rest. The signs need to be very simple. At the end, get the children to cut out their signs, and jumble them up. Then ask each child in turn to pick out one of his signs, and describe it to you clearly enough for you to reproduce it on the board or flipchart. Can the rest of the group work out what it means?

Tip

Children may already be familiar with some standard road signs, and it is quite acceptable for them to reproduce these; but they can invent their own if they prefer.

EXPLAINING & DESCRIBING

Stage I

Stage II

Stage III

Stage IV

Circle Time

Hall/PE

Literacy

Numeracy

Drama

Small Group

Art

Humanities

Science

Design Technology

PHSE

Food Technology

Time Travel (1)

Aim

To be able to describe the scenery, flora and fauna of a particular country, or area of a country, vividly and accurately.

Equipment

Names of countries or areas, written on individual slips or cards. Lists including all the names. (The places chosen will depend on work covered so far in Humanities.)

Activity

Put the individual place names into a hat or box. Give all the children a copy of the list of place names. Explain to the children that in turn they are going to be transported in a time machine to some other part of the world. They draw a place name out of the hat, and must describe it carefully until somebody thinks they can identify it from their list. Stress that descriptions can include plants, animals, people and buildings, as well as physical features and temperature. The traveller continues with his description until the place is guessed correctly.

Examples

The Arctic or Antarctica
A rainforest
A desert area
An African game reserve
The Alps

EXPLAINING & DESCRIBING

Stage I

Stage II

Stage III

Stage IV

Circle Time

Hall/PE

Literacy

Numeracy

Drama

Small Group

Art

Humanities

Science

Design Technology

PHSE

Food Technology

Inventors (1)

Aim

To be able to explain how a machine works.

Equipment

A clear picture of several different types of machine.

Preparation

Copy the machine pictures and enlarge if necessary. Put the children into groups of three or four. Give each group member a copy of their allocated machine picture. The children are to take their pictures home and, if possible, have a look at the real thing, – for example, a bicycle, before you play the game. Alternatively they can do some research through encyclopaedias or the internet.

Activity

Divide the children into their groups. Explain that they will have a few minutes in which to discuss the machine. They need to think about what the machine is for, and what it enables us to do that we could not do before (or what it enables us to do more efficiently). Where would it be useful? What are its moving parts? How do they work? (Energy sources such as electricity are taken for granted!) The groups then present 'their' machine, to the rest of the class, as a brand new invention, either holding up the picture, or demonstrating on the board or flipchart. They can do this either by delegating the task to a spokesperson, or by taking turns to contribute. The other children award the inventions marks out of five for usefulness, fun and sales potential. At the end, the class votes on which invention they would finance first.

Examples

Bicycle, crane, food processor, canal lock, traffic lights, lift, escalator, windmill, scales, camera, digger.

Tip

You might like to spread this game over several brief sessions.

EXPLAINING & DESCRIBING

Stage I

Stage II

Stage III

Stage IV

Circle Time

Hall/PE

Literacy

Numeracy

Drama

Small Group

Art

Humanities

Science

Design Technology

PHSE

Food Technology

Pantomime

Aim
To be able to describe a stage set for a well-known pantomime.

Equipment

None.

Preparation

Before playing this game, it is essential that all the children are familiar with a number of stories on which pantomimes are based.

Activity

Tell the children that they are going to be 'stage managers', and have to work out the set for a pantomime of their own choosing. Give them about five minutes to think about it, and to make notes if they wish. Then get each child in turn to describe his scene to you and the rest of the group. They may like to have a space cleared in which they can move about to indicate where pieces of furniture or other props go. In this case they may also want to borrow another child or children to be positioned appropriately. Encourage them to describe their stage set as graphically as possible. Each presentation earns a round of applause.

Example

Cinderella. The scene is a huge, old-fashioned castle kitchen. There is a small smoky fire smouldering away in the big fireplace. Cinderella is sitting by the fire, holding out her hands to try to get warm. She is dressed in a raggedy old grey dress, which is much too big for her. A black cat is sitting beside her…

EXPLAINING ≠ DESCRIBING

Stage I

Stage II

Stage III

Stage IV

Circle Time

Hall/PE

Literacy

Numeracy

Drama

Small Group

Art

Humanities

Science

Design Technology

PHSE

Food Technology

Time Travel (2)

Aim

To be able to describe the scenery, people and buildings (if any), at some time in the past.

Equipment

Times written on individual slips or cards. Lists of all the times.
(These need to be related to material already covered in Humanities.)

Activity

Put the individual slips into a hat or box. Give all the children a copy of the complete list of times. The game is played exactly like 'Time Travel' (1) but this time the children are to imagine they have gone back in time. One child at a time picks a slip out of the hat, and describes what he can see, hear and smell. He continues until somebody guesses correctly which time on the list is being described.

Example

A family group having a meal in the Stone Age
A scene in a Roman Villa
A country cottage during the Second World War
Children playing in Ancient Egypt
Sports in Ancient Greece
Florence Nightingale's hospital ward
Sir Francis Drake's ship.

Stage I

Stage II

Stage III

Stage IV

Circle Time

Hall/PE

Literacy

Numeracy

Drama

Small
Group

Art

Humanities

Science

Design
Technology

PHSE

Food
Technology

EXPLAINING & DESCRIBING

Salesman

Aim
To be able to describe something in such a way as to make it sound extremely desirable and attractive.

Equipment

List of examples below.

Activity

Divide the children into two teams. In turn, someone from each team stands up and tries to sell an item to the members of the opposite team. They must describe it in the most glowing terms, and do everything they can to persuade the opposing team that they would like to buy it. They have a minute in which to sell the item. The 'buyers' must vote as to whether they would be persuaded or not. The winning team is the one which makes the most sales.

Example

A sports car
An evening dress
A mountain bike
A computer game
A state-of-the-art television
A new mobile phone
A new house
Some amazing trainers
A racehorse
A bread-making machine.

Extension

Encourage some discussion after each presentation, in which the potential 'buyers' challenge the salesman. For example, for the sports car: How expensive is a service? How easy is it to get spare parts? How long before you can get me one?

EXPLAINING & DESCRIBING

Stage I

Stage II

Stage III

Stage IV

Circle Time

Hall/PE

Literacy

Numeracy

Drama

Small Group

Art

Humanities

Science

Design Technology

PHSE

Food Technology

Recruiting Officer

Aim
To be able to describe a job or profession.

Equipment

None.

Preparation

Make a note of the different jobs and professions. You may decide to allocate certain jobs to particular children, to let them choose for themselves, or to let them draw slips out of a hat, in order to randomise the choice.

Activity

Explain to the children that they are going to take turns to pretend to be a member of some trade or profession. They are going to tell everybody all the interesting and rewarding features of their jobs. They can talk about a whole day or a particular episode, as they wish. Can they fill their audience with enthusiasm for their chosen walk of life? Some jobs will have more instant appeal than others!

Examples

nurse	doctor
surgeon	firefighter
police officer	carpenter
plumber	farmer
shopkeeper	dentist
teacher	member of parliament
journalist	hairdresser
vet.	

Tip

Certain children may have knowledge of less familiar areas of work, and you may wish to let them choose these.

EXPLAINING & DESCRIBING

Stage I

Stage II

Stage III

Stage IV

Circle Time

Hall/PE

Literacy

Numeracy

Drama

Small Group

Art

Humanities

Science

Design Technology

PHSE

Food Technology

Inventors (2)

Aim
To be able to describe a gadget that the children themselves have invented and drawn.

Equipment

Paper and pencils.

Activity

Explain to the children that they are inventors who are going to be asked to think up and draw some gadgets that are urgently needed. Each child will be designing a different invention. Allow the children up to 10 minutes to complete the drawings. Then everybody gets a chance to explain their invention and how it works. Encourage the rest of the group to ask questions. You may need to prompt them to ask more detailed questions, such as 'What if the string isn't strong enough?'

Examples

A robot that will make cups of tea.
A chair that turns into a bed.
A gadget for picking up clothes off the floor.
A machine for keeping your plate on the table in space.
A way of keeping ice lollies cold while you play on the Playstation.

Understanding & Using Spoken Language
USING SPOKEN LANGUAGE

REPORTING &
DEBATING

Stage I

Stage II

Stage III

Stage IV

Circle Time

Hall/PE

Literacy

Numeracy

Drama

Small Group

Art

Humanities

Science

Design Technology

PHSE

Food Technology

REPORTING & DEBATING

Warm-Ups for Reporting and Debating

Twister

Everyone needs to stand in a space big enough to stretch out their arms horizontally without touching anyone else. Stand with feet about a shoulders' width apart. Raise both arms out sideways at shoulder height. Bend the right arm so that fingers lightly touch the back of your head. At the same time bend the left arm so that backs of the fingers lightly touch the small of your back. With arms in this position twist upper body slowly to the left. Twist back again extending arms sideways at the same time. Repeat to the other side. Do this action three times on each side.

String it Along

This is a sentence-making activity for a group of up to eight children. If the group is bigger than this you may need to split it into two smaller groups. Start with a noun and its determiner – for example, *The dog, A cat*. The next person has to add a word or a short phrase. Continue in this way until everyone in the group has made a contribution.

Example
The dog – with long ears – ran – down the path – but – when he saw – the cat – he stopped.

REPORTING & DEBATING

Stage I

Stage II

Stage III

Stage IV

Circle Time

Hall/PE

Literacy

Numeracy

Drama

Small Group

Art

Humanities

Science

Design Technology

PHSE

Food Technology

Make an Adventure

Aim
To be able to make a verbal prediction.

Equipment

A large sheet of paper, pencils.

Preparation

Divide the paper into sections. You also need to prepare the opening sentence for a story (see example).

Activity

Tell the children that you are going to make up a story together. Read them an opening sentence, then ask the first child what happened next. Draw a sketch of this in the first box. You then continue the story by adding a choice of two alternatives for what happens next. The next child chooses what happened, which you draw in the next box. Repeat by adding two more alternatives. Carry on until all the boxes are filled. The final challenge is to see if anyone can tell the whole story.

Example

While Peter was out walking he found a doorway in a stone wall.
(You then say: 'When he pushed it, he found it was open. Did he (a) turn round and run home; or (b) go through the door?')

Extension

The story could be written as a creative writing activity. It could also be turned into a drama.

Stage I

Stage II

Stage III

Stage IV

Circle Time

Hall/PE

Literacy

Numeracy

Drama

Small Group

Art

Humanities

Science

Design Technology

PHSE

Food Technology

REPORTING & DEBATING

Finish the Story

Aim
To be able to identify appropriate endings to stories, and relate them.

Equipment

Short stories from Teaching Resources (pages 249–250). Alternative story endings, written on slips of paper. A bag or box.

How to Play

Choose one of the stories, and put the alternative endings for that story on slips of paper in the bag or box. Explain to the children that you are going to tell them a story, and they are going to help you choose different ways in which the story might end. Some of the endings will not do at all! You tell the story up to the last cliff-hanging moment, and then choose a child to come and draw one of the endings out of the bag. If the child can read, they read the ending out to the class. If not, teacher whispers it to them, and they repeat it to the class. The group votes on whether it is a good, silly or inappropriate ending. Continue until everyone has had a turn. The children could then try to finish the story themselves.

Example

'An aeroplane comes down on a remote mountainside. One of the crew sets off to fetch help. He trudges through the snowy forest, and at long last, when he is nearly exhausted, he sees in front of him...'
- a little house with lights shining out
- a railway track
- a swimming costume
- another aeroplane with the key in the ignition

REPORTING & DEBATING

Newsreel (1)

Aim
To be able to recount events using the past tense.

Equipment

A collection of pictures from newspapers and magazines, depicting some kind of action or event.

How to Play

Show the children the pictures first, and talk about what is happening in each picture. Then tell them that they are going to take turns to pretend to 'read the news' to the rest of the class. Each child selects a picture, and gives a short account of what happened. You may like to give scores for information, clarity, use of the past tense, and how interesting the report was.

Stage I

Stage II

Stage III

Stage IV

Circle Time

Hall/PE

Literacy

Numeracy

Drama

Small Group

Art

Humanities

Science

Design Technology

PHSE

Food Technology

Stage I

Stage II

Stage III

Stage IV

Circle Time

Hall/PE

Literacy

Numeracy

Drama

Small Group

Art

Humanities

Science

Design Technology

PHSE

Food Technology

REPORTING & DEBATING

Television Times

Aim
To be able to tell what happened in a television programme or film.

Equipment

None.

How to Play

Divide the children into two teams. The idea of the game is that a child from one team starts to describe a recent television programme or film. As soon as anyone in the opposing team thinks they can guess what the programme or film is, they call it out. If they are wrong, the narrator carries on. If they are right, one of that team has a turn to be the narrator, and so on, until as many people as possible have had a go.

Tip

Children often find it extraordinarily difficult to grasp that they must not *name* the film or programme. You will have to emphasise this. They will soon discover that naming the principal actors or game show hosts is also an immediate give-away.

Extension

You can make this game much harder by telling the narrators to try to go on as long as possible before the opposing team guesses correctly. The game can also be played about books or stories, provided you know that everybody is familiar with the books chosen.

REPORTING & DEBATING

Stage I

Stage II

Stage III

Stage IV

Circle Time

Hall/PE

Literacy

Numeracy

Drama

Small Group

Art

Humanities

Science

Design Technology

PHSE

Food Technology

Missing Middles

Aim
To be able to invent and relate the missing part of a story, after being given the beginning and the end.

Equipment

None.

How to Play

Pretend to the children that you have found an old book. The beginnings and ends of some stories are there, but the pages with the middle sections have been torn out. You are going to tell them some of the beginnings and endings, and you would like them to fill in the middle bits. Divide the children into four groups. You will ask each group in turn for ideas which should follow on one from another.

Example

'A boy looks out of his bedroom window as night is falling, and sees a dragon landing in the garden…The boy looks around the strange planet in amazement.'

Extension

You might like to write up the best of the resulting stories, and let the children illustrate it. You can also use this activity as a basis for the children's own story-writing.

Stage I

Stage II

Stage III

Stage IV

Circle Time

Hall/PE

Literacy

Numeracy

Drama

Small
Group

Art

Humanities

Science

Design
Technology

PHSE

Food
Technology

REPORTING & DEBATING

Crystal Ball

Aim
To be able to predict consequences to actions verbally.

Equipment

A bean-bag.

Preparation

You need to make a list of real life situations that the children can make a sensible prediction about. (This could be linked to topic work or PHSE – see examples below.) Write the situations on pieces of paper – you need one for each member of the group.

How to Play

Everyone stands in a circle. A 'situation' sheet is stuck on each person's back. One child is chosen to start the activity, and they stand in the middle of the circle with their eyes shut. The bean-bag is then passed silently around the group until the child in the middle says 'Stop!'. The child holding the bean-bag turns around to reveal the situation on his back. The child in the middle has to try to predict a plausible outcome to the situation. When they have done this, the child holding the bean-bag takes their place and the game continues.

Example

It didn't rain for a whole year.
What if you only ate sweets and crisps, and drank Coke?
What if children could choose whether they wanted to go to school or not?
What if everybody dropped their litter on the ground?

Tip

You may need to help the children read the sheets.

REPORTING & DEBATING

Stage I

Stage II

Stage III

Stage IV

Circle Time

Hall/PE

Literacy

Numeracy

Drama

Small Group

Art

Humanities

Science

Design Technology

PHSE

Food Technology

Dangerous Mission

Aim
To be able to make predictions based on a few given facts, or to risk making a guess.

Equipment

'Dangerous Mission' story and list of answers from Teaching Resources (pages 251–252).

Preparation

Photocopy and cut out the answers to the predictions or guesses. Fold the slips over and number them clearly as indicated. Spread them out on the table so that the numbers can be seen.

How to Play

This game is for three to four children. Tell the group that you are following behind some adventurers who are seeking hidden treasure. Every now and then they come to a particularly dangerous moment or have to face a particularly difficult decision. The children are to predict or guess what decision the treasure-seekers will make. They take turns. After each prediction or guess, the child who made it picks up an answer slip, in number order, and reads what it says. Were they right? The story then continues to the next moment of decision. Give as much help with reading as necessary.

Tip

Where the child's choice or alternatives can be based on facts rather than guesswork, encourage discussion as to the reason for their choice.

REPORTING & DEBATING

Stage I

Stage II

Stage III

Stage IV

Circle Time

Hall/PE

Literacy

Numeracy

Drama

Small Group

Art

Humanities

Science

Design Technology

PHSE

Food Technology

Newsreel (2)

Aim
To be able to construct a coherent news report from jumbled pieces of information, and read it out clearly.

Equipment

'Newsreel' stories from Teaching Resources (page 253).

Preparation

Copy and cut out enough news flashes for the number of teams or children playing.

Activity

This game can be played by two teams, with readers coming alternately from each team. Tell the children that they will be given a collection of news flashes, coming in over the radio or internet from all over the world. Their job is to work as a group to put the news flashes together and make a clear news story. They then read the story out to the audience. They can add their own words to the news flashes to make the report more exciting, moving or interesting.

Example

Fire at sea. Crew all safe. Huge oil tanker ablaze. Captain missing. Crews took to lifeboats. Rescued by cruise liner. Ship sinking. Captain taken off by helicopter.

Extension

Play this as a competition, and ask the audience to award points out of 10 to each reader. Encourage debate over the awarding of points, and see who emerges as the 'News Reporter of the Year'.

REPORTING & DEBATING

Stage I

Stage II

Stage III

Stage IV

Circle Time

Hall/PE

Literacy

Numeracy

Drama

Small Group

Art

Humanities

Science

Design Technology

PHSE

Food Technology

Question Time

Aim
To be able to generate questions about a specific topic.

Equipment

None.

Activity

Choose a child to start the activity off. They must tell the group something that happened recently, either at school or at home. Each member of the group then has to ask a different question about the information given. Questions should be recorded either on paper, a flipchart or a tape recorder. When everyone has had a turn count how many different questions were asked. The activity can be repeated if there is time.

Extension

This activity could be linked to topic work, where appropriate.

Stage I

Stage II

Stage III

Stage IV

Circle Time

Hall/PE

Literacy

Numeracy

Drama

Small Group

Art

Humanities

Science

Design Technology

PHSE

Food Technology

REPORTING & DEBATING

What Next?

Aim
To be able to predict the end of a story.

Equipment

'What Next' texts from Teaching Resources (page 254). Paper and pencils.

How to Play

Tell the children you are going to read them a short story, but explain that the person who wrote the story was interrupted, and never finished it. Give everyone a piece of paper and a pencil. If possible, seat them so that they cannot copy anyone else's picture. When they have listened to the story, they have to think of an ending and draw it on the sheet of paper. When everyone has finished the drawing, each child takes a turn at telling their ending.

Extension

The main story could be printed, and each child's version of the ending inserted, to make a number of similar stories with different endings. Each child could type their ending on a computer, save the whole story, and add illustrations.

REPORTING & DEBATING

	Stage I
	Stage II
	Stage III
	Stage IV
	Circle Time
	Hall/PE
	Literacy
	Numeracy
	Drama
	Small Group
	Art
	Humanities
	Science
	Design Technology
	PHSE
	Food Technology

Me Please!

Aim
To be able to give convincing reasons why you should be the one to have a particular treat, privilege or responsibility.

Equipment

None.

Preparation

Write down a list of imaginary treats, privileges or responsibilities.

Activity

Explain to the children that you are going to tell them about certain imaginary treats, privileges or responsibilities that they might like to have. You will choose people to try to convince the class that they should be the ones to have these treats or privileges. Read out one of the 'treats', and ask for hands up. Choose someone to stand up and give as many good reasons as they can why they should be the lucky one. About a minute each is probably enough.

Example

To take a small puppy home for the weekend, and look after it.
To have some football coaching from David Beckham.
To have a whole day in school when you can choose what to do, such as art, craft, music, or sport.

Stage I

Stage II

Stage III

Stage IV

Circle Time

Hall/PE

Literacy

Numeracy

Drama

Small Group

Art

Humanities

Science

Design Technology

PHSE

Food Technology

REPORTING & DEBATING

Text!

Aim
To be able to condense a message into a minimum number of crucial words.

Equipment

'Text!' messages from Teaching Resources (page 255), written on slips of paper.

Activity

Divide the children into two teams. Explain that you are going to give them some urgent messages. These have to be sent very quickly, and every word costs a lot of money. They must express the message in as few words as possible. Team A works out its message, and then reads it to Team B. If Team B understands the message Team A wins. However, they lose one point from a starter of 20 for every unnecessary word used. Then swap over.

Example

'A man has fallen over the cliff near Swanage. We think he has broken his leg.
He is conscious, but in pain. Scramble the helicopter as soon as possible.
('Man on cliff Swanage. Conscious, leg broken, pain. Helicopter urgent.)

REPORTING & DEBATING

Stage I

Stage II

Stage III

Stage IV

Circle Time

Hall/PE

Literacy

Numeracy

Drama

Small Group

Art

Humanities

Science

Design Technology

PHSE

Food Technology

At The Scene

Aim
To be able to construct a brief spoken report to match a picture.

Equipment

A collection of pictures cut from national newspapers.

Preparation

Number each of the pictures. There should be at least one for each child in the group.

Activity

The children have to make up a brief 'report' to match a picture from a newspaper. Demonstrate the activity by selecting one of the pictures and making up a sentence or two to match it. Try to word it as if it were from a real newspaper. Number each child in the group. Put the pictures out on the table. Each child selects the picture that corresponds to their number. Allow them a few minutes to work out what to say. Then seat everyone in a circle. Choose a child to start the reporting. They hold up their picture and give their report. Continue round the circle until everyone has had a turn.

REPORTING & DEBATING

Stage I

Stage II

Stage III

Stage IV

Circle Time

Hall/PE

Literacy

Numeracy

Drama

Small Group

Art

Humanities

Science

Design Technology

PHSE

Food Technology

Tell Us!

Aim
To be able to describe a place and an event clearly and with some dramatic effect.

Equipment

None.

Preparation

Jot down a list of places and events.

Activity

This activity can be carried out as a competitive team game in which the teams collect points, or individually. Explain to the children that you are going to give each of them in turn a place and event to describe. They have to keep going for one minute. You will be awarding points for clarity of description, facts given, and atmosphere created. The latter may be by use of appropriate adjectives, and dramatic delivery.

Examples

Going to: a circus; a funfair; a zoo; an airport; a sealife centre; a big railway station; a football, cricket, or rugby match; a street market; a theatre; a cinema; a planetarium; Madame Tussaud's; the Tower of London or a theme park.

Extension

Extend the time given to two minutes or more.

REPORTING & DEBATING

Stage I

Stage II

Stage III

Stage IV

Circle Time

Hall/PE

Literacy

Numeracy

Drama

Small Group

Art

Humanities

Science

Design Technology

PHSE

Food Technology

Celebrity

Aim
To be able to turn a list of items into a spoken account.

Equipment

'Celebrity' lists from Teaching Resources (page 256).

Preparation

Make copies of the lists, and cut them into individual sheets.

Activity

This is an activity for a group of not more than five children. Put the lists face down on the table. Ask one child to select a list. Together, read the items on the list. You may need to do this more than once. Then designate a particular item to each child. They have to make up a sentence which conveys the information. Each child in the group takes a turn at saying their sentence. You can then act as a television presenter and introduce your celebrity, using the sentences the children have made up.

Extension

The children can act as presenter.

Stage I

Stage II

Stage III

Stage IV

Circle Time

Hall/PE

Literacy

Numeracy

Drama

Small
Group

Art

Humanities

Science

Design
Technology

PHSE

Food
Technology

REPORTING & DEBATING

Advertisements

Aim
To be able to make up a persuasive text.

Equipment

A selection of everyday items – for example, chocolate bars, washing powder, biscuits, gel pens, trainers.

Activity

Explain to the children that they have to make up a slogan to 'sell' an item from the selection. Divide them into pairs. Each pair appoints a scribe and a spokesman. They must then make a slogan containing not more than three sentences. Allow about five minutes for planning time. Each pair then presents their advertisement.

Extension

The children could make posters showing their advertisement.

REPORTING &
DEBATING

Stage I

Stage II

Stage III

Stage IV

Circle Time

Hall/PE

Literacy

Numeracy

Drama

Small
Group

Art

Humanities

Science

Design
Technology

PHSE

Food
Technology

On The Spot

Aim
To be able to ask a series of relevant questions.

Equipment

None.

Preparation

Choose a number of well-known book or media characters with whom the children will be familiar. Write them on separate cards.

Activity

The idea is for each child to ask the person a relevant question. Choose a child to be the first 'on the spot'. Give them one of the character cards. Make sure they are familiar with the character. Tell the rest of the group that they are the studio audience, and they will have the chance to ask a well-known character some questions. Then, acting as the host, introduce the character. For example, 'We are very lucky to have Harry Potter in the studio tonight!' The children then take turns to ask relevant questions. Encourage them to listen to each other, as one question can lead to another. Make a note of the questions and answers, then when everyone has had a turn you can feed back the information obtained.

Stage I

Stage II

Stage III

Stage IV

Circle Time

Hall/PE

Literacy

Numeracy

Drama

Small Group

Art

Humanities

Science

Design Technology

PHSE

Food Technology

REPORTING & DEBATING

Troubleshooter

Aim
To be able to express different ways of resolving a problem.

Equipment

'Troubleshooter' problems from Teaching Resources (page 257).

Preparation

Copy the problems and cut them out into individual cards.

Activity

Choose one of the 'problems'. One child reads it out to the group. Divide the group into pairs. Each pair works out a solution to the problem. Allow about five minutes for this. Then one person from each pair feeds back their solution to the rest of the group. Write the solutions on the whiteboard or flipchart.

Speechmark

REPORTING & DEBATING

Stage I

Stage II

Stage III

Stage IV

Circle Time

Hall/PE

Literacy

Numeracy

Drama

Small Group

Art

Humanities

Science

Design Technology

PHSE

Food Technology

Persuaders

Aim
To be able to use spoken language persuasively.

Equipment

List of 'Persuader' statements from Teaching Resources (page 258).

Preparation

Copy the statements and cut them up into individual cards.

Activity

Divide the children into Team A and Team B. The opposing teams sit or stand facing each other. Give the first person in Team A a statement, which they read out. Their opposite number from Team B disagrees with the statement and has to persuade the Team A member to change their mind. You may like to lay down ground rules before you start such as 'only one person can talk at a time', or 'put your hand up before you speak.'

REPORTING &
DEBATING

Stage I
Stage II
Stage III
Stage IV
Circle Time
Hall/PE
Literacy
Numeracy
Drama
Small Group
Art
Humanities
Science
Design Technology
PHSE
Food Technology

Twenty Questions

Aim
To be able to guess the identity of a person by careful questioning.

Equipment

None.

Activity

Divide the class into two. Explain that you are going to tell one group the name of a person. It may be somebody alive or dead, British or from overseas. They may be – or may have been – rulers; politicians; soldiers; sailors or airmen; actors or singers; authors; sports stars; musicians; or people from one of the professions, such as medicine. The members of the second group have to ask questions which will gradually lead them to the right answer. You will need to start them off by demonstrating the kind of question allowed, which must be able to be answered by a 'Yes' or a 'No'. They can have twenty questions.

Example

Admiral Nelson: Is he alive? (No) Is he British? (Yes) Did he live a long time ago? (Yes) Have we learnt about him? (Yes/No) Was he a hero? (Yes) Was he a soldier? (No), etc...

Tips

The children may well not guess right at all for the first few times you play this game.
Of course you will choose personalities with which you know the children are familiar.

REPORTING & DEBATING

| Stage I |
| Stage II |
| Stage III |
| **Stage IV** |
| **Circle Time** |
| Hall/PE |
| **Literacy** |
| Numeracy |
| **Drama** |
| **Small Group** |
| Art |
| Humanities |
| Science |
| Design Technology |
| PHSE |
| Food Technology |

Debate It

Aim

To be able to present the pros and cons of a simple proposition, and to be able to weigh up the merits of both sides of the argument.

Equipment

None.

Activity

Before attempting this activity, the children will have to be introduced to the idea of debating issues, and, if possible, have seen or heard some part of a debate. Explain the procedure to the children, then tell them what the first issue for debate is going to be. All together, brainstorm the pros and cons of the argument, with the adult keeping a note of the points raised. Give one child a list of the pros, and another child a list of the cons. The activity itself takes place a day or so later, when the two children have had time to put their arguments in order. They may choose to work from a script, notes, or from memory. A vote is taken at the end.

Examples

Compulsory school uniform is a good idea.
Schools should ban crisps and sweets on school premises.
People who misbehave at football matches should lose their passports for 10 years.
Zoos are a good idea.
Circuses are cruel, and should be closed down.
Everybody should learn a foreign language.

Extension

Appoint two advocates to propose and oppose a motion without the prior brainstorm.

Stage I

Stage II

Stage III

Stage IV

Circle Time

Hall/PE

Literacy

Numeracy

Drama

Small Group

Art

Humanities

Science

Design Technology

PHSE

Food Technology

REPORTING & DEBATING

Survey

Aim

To be able to ask appropriate questions to elicit the desired answer, and to report on findings.

Equipment

None.

Preparation

Jot down a list of topics for statistics, which the children are going to have to find out.

Activity

This activity is best for not more than about 10 children. Explain that they are going to carry out a survey, or census. They will all be given something to find out. To get the answers, they will have to question everyone in the group. They will need to make a note of who they have asked, and put the answers beside the names. When they have questioned everybody, they need to add up the numbers they have collected, divide by the number of people questioned, and come up with an average. In turn they will report their findings to the group.

Example

One child will be told to ask how many brothers, if any, each child has. Another will ask how many sisters, or how many pets, or how many children under three in the family. As well as producing averages, the children will be able to compare the different statistics they have collected.

REPORTING & DEBATING

Boardroom

Aim
To understand the roles of members of a committee and be able to select them.

Equipment

None

Preparation

Make an individual card for each of the various possible 'outings'.

Activity

Divide the children into groups of six or more. Explain the roles of a chairman and a clerk or secretary. Give the children a minute to elect a chairman and a secretary, bearing in mind that the secretary needs to have reasonable writing skills. Then distribute an 'outing' slip to all the 'committee members', apart from the chairmen and secretaries. Tell the chairmen that they are to let everybody have a turn to put forward reasons why the class should go on the outing they have on their slip. He must keep control, make sure everybody has a turn, and stop people calling out, interrupting, or talking for too long. The secretary notes down two or three good points from each speaker. When the chairmen think their group has had long enough to put forward their points of view (say five minutes), the secretaries recap the ideas from their notes. The group then takes a vote on the preferred outing. The chairmen report back to the whole class the decisions they have reached.

Example

Possible outings: A pantomime; an overnight camping trip; a visit to France; a lesson in abseiling; a lesson in canoeing; a visit to Windsor Castle.

Tip

This activity is unlikely to go smoothly or according to plan! The most valuable part of the exercise will probably be the general discussion about what went wrong.

Stage I

Stage II

Stage III

Stage IV

Circle Time

Hall/PE

Literacy

Numeracy

Drama

Small Group

Art

Humanities

Science

Design Technology

PHSE

Food Technology

REPORTING & DEBATING

Stage I

Stage II

Stage III

Stage IV

Circle Time

Hall/PE

Literacy

Numeracy

Drama

Small Group

Art

Humanities

Science

Design Technology

PHSE

Food Technology

Point of View

Aim
To be able to communicate an opinion coherently.

Equipment

'Points of View' headlines and presenter cards from Teaching Resources (page 259).

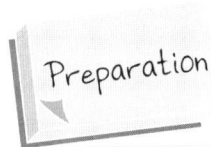

Preparation

Photocopy the 'headline' and 'presenter' cards and cut them out.

Activity

This activity is suitable for a group of up to eight children. Divide the group into two teams. Each group should work in separate parts of the room. Put the headline up so that everyone can see it. Read it out, and make sure both teams understand what it means. Give each team a different 'presenter' card. Tell them they have to talk about the headline from the point of view of their 'presenter'. Allow a few minutes for each team to appoint a spokesman and to sort out what they are going to say. Then each team reports the headline. When they have finished, they have to try to decide on the occupation of the opposing team. You will probably need to show them both occupations.

USING SPEECH EFFECTIVELY

USING SPEECH
EFFECTIVELY

Stage I

Stage II

Stage III

Stage IV

Circle Time

Hall/PE

Literacy

Numeracy

Drama

Small
Group

Art

Humanities

Science

Design
Technology

PHSE

Food
Technology

Warm Ups for Using Speech Effectively

Tongue-Twister

Below is a selection of tongue-twisters. You may like to learn them together at first, and then allow individual children to have a go.

- Black bug bit a big black bear. But where is the big black bear that the big black bug bit?
- A big bug bit the little beetle but the little beetle bit the big bug back.
- If two witches were watching two watches, which witch would watch which watch?
- Red leather, yellow leather, red leather, yellow leather, red leather, yellow leather;...
- Red lorry, yellow lorry, red lorry, yellow lorry, red lorry, yellow lorry;...
- Six shimmering sharks sharply striking shins.
- Leaping lizards like to lick lovely lemon lollipops for lunch.
- What noise annoys an oyster most? A noisy noise annoys an oyster most.
- She shuts the shop shutters, so the shopping shoppers can't shop.
- I can think of thin things, six thin things, can you?
  Yes, I can think of six thin things, and of six thick things too.

Compliments

Sit in a circle. Each person pays a compliment to the person on their left. Make sure everyone knows what a compliment is and give examples if necessary. You may need to help them 'frame' their compliment by suggesting everyone starts with 'I like X because ...'

Speechmark

Stage I

Stage II

Stage III

Stage IV

Circle Time

Hall/PE

Literacy

Numeracy

Drama

Small Group

Art

Humanities

Science

Design Technology

PHSE

Food Technology

USING SPEECH EFFECTIVELY

Volume Control (1)

Aim
To be able to vary the volume of the voice to suit spoken material.

Equipment

'Volume Control' short paragraphs from Teaching Resources (pages 260–261).

Preparation

Copy several of the short paragraphs, enough for each group to have one.

Activity

Divide the children into groups of at least four. Explain that this game uses their volume controls – like the loud and soft controls with which they are familiar on televisions, tape recorders or radios. Separate the groups into 'volume up' and 'volume down' groups. In turn, the groups read their passages aloud in unison, raising or lowering their volume controls on the parts indicated. Loud parts are marked in bold type, quiet parts in italics. Then swap around so that each group has a turn at being 'volume up' or 'volume down'.

Example

As the children went into the cave, they could hear a distant booming – **boom, boom, boom**. The goblins were hammering. The children's feet rang on the stones – **clang, clang** – and they were afraid the goblins would hear them. As they got nearer, the **whooshing** sound of the waterfall grew louder and louder.

Tip

You could read the text line by line for poor readers, and get the child to repeat.

Extension

Give the groups passages to read in which they have both to raise and lower the volume. Give them unmarked passages, and let them work out in groups where to increase, and where to decrease, the volume.

Stage I

Stage II

Stage III

Stage IV

Circle Time

Hall/PE

Literacy

Numeracy

Drama

Small Group

Art

Humanities

Science

Design Technology

PHSE

Food Technology

USING SPEECH EFFECTIVELY

Moody (1)

Aim

To be able to match tone of voice and speed of delivery to sad or solemn texts.

Equipment

'Moody (1)' brief texts from Teaching Resources (pages 262–263).

Preparation

Copy and cut out a sad or solemn text for everyone taking part. Talk about the way in which both prose and poetry may be written to induce an atmosphere – repeated single syllables to produce a gloomy feeling, and multisyllabic words and a pattern of light stresses and unvoiced sounds to express cheerfulness.

Activity

Restrict this activity to about eight or 10 children. In turn, the children stand up, either in front of the group or in the middle of a circle, and read out their passages. Remind them to slow down and make their voices sad or serious as they go along. Give everybody a clap.

Example

It was a sad, sad day when Arthur's gerbil died. That morning the rain poured down steadily, the sky was dark grey, and Arthur's heart was as heavy as lead. He buried poor old Whiffles in the garden, under an apple tree, and placed a stone over him saying: 'Here lies Whiffles. A long-lost friend'.

Tips

Read one of the texts yourself first, exaggerating the slow pace, to give the children the idea. Help poor readers by saying the text line by line for them to repeat.

Extension

Select some passages from story books, and challenge the children to judge where to slow down.

USING SPEECH EFFECTIVELY

Good or Bad News?

Aim

To be able to alter the tone of one's voice to convey emotion.

Equipment

List of announcements (see examples below).

Preparation

Write out each announcement twice on separate small cards. Draw a smiley face on one of each pair, and a sad face on the other. Shuffle the cards.

Activity

The group stands in a line, side by side. Choose one child to start. Give them the card and make sure they can read the message. A smiley face on the card indicates that the child should announce good news; a sad face, bad news. They then stand behind the line of children and announce the message, using their tone of voice to match the emotion. The next child in the line has to say whether it is good or bad news. Continue until everyone has had a turn.

Example

Guess what!
Come quickly!
I've got some news.
Something has happened!
Listen very carefully.
This is an important announcement.
I have something to tell you all.
Everyone line up immediately.
This was found in the entrance hall.
Everyone in Year 4 must go to the office.

| Stage I |
| Stage II |
| Stage III |
| Stage IV |
| Circle Time |
| Hall/PE |
| Literacy |
| Numeracy |
| Drama |
| Small Group |
| Art |
| Humanities |
| Science |
| Design Technology |
| PHSE |
| Food Technology |

Stage I

Stage II

Stage III

Stage IV

Circle Time

Hall/PE

Literacy

Numeracy

Drama

Small Group

Art

Humanities

Science

Design Technology

PHSE

Food Technology

USING SPEECH EFFECTIVELY

Double Spinner

Aim
To be able to give clearly audible instructions to someone out of sight.

Equipment

Raceboard (page 198) and 'Double Spinner' template from Teaching Resources (page 264).
Die and counters.

Preparation

Copy the spinner template onto card and mark it as follows: +1, -1, +2, -2, +3, -3, +4, -4. Assemble by pushing a short pencil, or similar sharp object, through the middle.

Activity

This is a game for no more than four players. It is played as a simple race game. The rules regarding the star, happy and sad squares must be agreed on before you start – see example below. Choose a child to start. They must sit with their back to the game, and spin the spinner without anyone else seeing. They then tell the player how to move – for example, 'Move three spaces forwards.' If the player lands on a marked square, they must tell the 'spinner' which type of square it is. The 'spinner' then gives the appropriate instruction. The player then becomes the 'spinner', and gives instructions to the next child. Continue until the race is won. The further away from the game the 'spinners' sit the more clearly they will have to speak their instructions.

Example

Star   = Take another turn
Happy face = Move forward one space
Sad face   = Move back one space

USING SPEECH EFFECTIVELY

Stage I

Stage II

Stage III

Stage IV

Circle Time

Hall/PE

Literacy

Numeracy

Drama

Small Group

Art

Humanities

Science

Design Technology

PHSE

Food Technology

Whisperer

Aim

To be able to give a clear message in a whisper.

Equipment

'Whisperer' messages from Teaching Resources (page 265).

Preparation

Copy the messages onto card, and cut into individual cards.

Activity

The children stand in a line one behind the other. You stand opposite the first child in the line, at a distance. The first child steps forward and takes a card. If necessary help them read it. They then have to face the next child in the line, and whisper the message. If that child can repeat the message correctly, the 'whisperer' gets a point and moves to the back of the queue. If they cannot whisper the message correctly, help them but do not award a point. The next child comes forward and takes a card, whispers the message, and so on, until everyone has had a turn. You can play as many rounds as time allows. Points may be deducted for 'whisperers' who speak aloud rather than whispering. The children might start with five points and keep their own score, relating how many they have left when the game ends.

Stage I

Stage II

Stage III

Stage IV

Circle Time

Hall/PE

Literacy

Numeracy

Drama

Small Group

Art

Humanities

Science

Design Technology

PHSE

Food Technology

USING SPEECH EFFECTIVELY

Express Train

Aim
To be able to vary speed of speech.

Equipment

'Express Train' sounds and instructions in Teaching Resources (page 266).

Activity

Explain to the children that you are going to teach them some 'train noises'. First you are going to practise saying them all together. Later you will divide the children into two or more groups. These will either make the same sounds starting at different times (in the manner of a round or catch), or at different speeds; or they will make different noises. When they are divided up, they must concentrate hard on sticking to their own group's sound, and try not to be distracted by what the other group or groups are saying.

Examples

Trickety-track
Clickety-clack

USING SPEECH EFFECTIVELY

Stage I

Stage II

Stage III

Stage IV

Circle Time

Hall/PE

Literacy

Numeracy

Drama

Small Group

Art

Humanities

Science

Design Technology

PHSE

Food Technology

Volume Control (2)

Aim

To be able to adapt the volume of the voice to the proximity of the audience.

Equipment

'Volume Control (2)' short pieces of text from Teaching Resources (page 267).

Preparation

Print out the texts in large double-spaced type.

Activity

Arrange the class in three rows, one row near the speaker, one row two or three metres further back, and the last row a little further away still. Explain to the children that you want them to learn to adjust their volume controls so that their voice is pitched just right for their listeners. Give your first speaker a brief practice with one sentence: first say it so that the front row can just hear it, but nobody else can. Then raise the volume so that the first two rows can hear it comfortably; and finally pitch the voice so that everybody right at the back can hear. Choose a child to read first, and place him out in front of the class. Give him five or six texts in random order. They are marked 'front', 'middle' or 'back' to indicate the level of volume needed. He is to read one out, pitching his voice as indicated. He then awaits a response from his audience. If he has pitched his voice correctly, he will get a response either from the front row, the front two rows, or the whole group. Repeat with another speaker. It is not very easy either for the adult or the children to get this all right!

Example

Front: A magic ice-cream van has just pulled up outside the school. In a minute, the driver will come in with a box full of cornettos®, choc ices, 99 flakes®, and tubs. If anyone would like an ice-cream, say 'Yes!' now.

Stage I

Stage II

Stage III

Stage IV

Circle Time

Hall/PE

Literacy

Numeracy

Drama

Small Group

Art

Humanities

Science

Design Technology

PHSE

Food Technology

USING SPEECH EFFECTIVELY

Moody (2)

Aim
To be able to match tone of voice and speed of delivery to cheerful texts, and texts describing fast-moving events.

Equipment

'Moody (2)' brief texts from Teaching Resources (pages 268–269).

Preparation

Copy and cut out a different text for everyone taking part. Remind the children of the activity, 'Moody (1)', and the way in which tone of voice and speed of delivery can indicate sadness or cheerfulness. The texts for 'Moody (2)' are cheerful ones, and sometimes indicate fast-moving action, so the children need to remember that parts of the text may need to be taken quite fast.

Activity

This is an activity for up to eight children. The children stand up in turn, either in front of the group or in the middle of a circle, and read out their passage. Remind them to keep the pace up, and make their voice cheerful, as they go along.

Example

Pippa was so excited about her birthday party. The room where the tea was laid out was prettily decorated, with pink and purple balloons and paper streamers. Cakes, sandwiches and jellies were all ready. Peeping out of the window, Pippa thought she saw the first people arriving. Her mum was still in her bedroom, putting on her party clothes. Pippa ran to the bottom of the stairs and called up, 'Mum! Quick! Hurry up! People are coming!'

Tips

Read one of the texts yourself first, exaggerating the parts where you speed up, to give the children an example. Say the text line-by-line for poor readers, and give others help as needed.

Speechmark Ⓟ This page may be photocopied for instructional use only.
Understanding & Using Spoken Language © C Delamain & J Spring 2004

USING SPEECH EFFECTIVELY

Stage I

Stage II

Stage III

Stage IV

Circle Time

Hall/PE

Literacy

Numeracy

Drama

Small Group

Art

Humanities

Science

Design Technology

PHSE

Food Technology

Beat Out the Rhythm

Aim
To be able to detect the rhythm in a piece of verse, and recite the piece marking the rhythm clearly in the delivery. To understand the terms 'rhythm', 'stress' and 'syllable'.

Equipment
'Beat Out the Rhythm' limericks from Teaching Resources (pages 270–271).

Preparation
Copy a limerick for each child taking part, with the stressed syllables indicated in bold type.

Activity
Explain to the children that all limericks share a very similar rhythm. Read them one, exaggerating the stressed syllables, so that the rhythm is obvious. Tell them that they are each going to read out a limerick, fitting the words into the pattern that you have modelled. The bold type indicates where the stresses should fall.

Example
There **was** a young lady from **Ryde**,
Who ate **for**ty green **app**les and **died**.
The **app**les fer**ment**ed in**side** the la**ment**ed,
And made **ci**der in**side** her in**side**.

Tips
It may be necessary to explain some of the vocabulary in the limericks, so as to be sure that the children understand the humour.

USING SPEECH EFFECTIVELY

Stage I

Stage II

Stage III

Stage IV

Circle Time

Hall/PE

Literacy

Numeracy

Drama

Small Group

Art

Humanities

Science

Design Technology

PHSE

Food Technology

Messengers (1)

Aim
To be able to adapt style of speaking to suit different listeners.

Equipment

'Messengers (1)' characters and messages from Teaching Resources (page 272).

Preparation

Make cards with the names of the characters written on them, four of each.
Copy and cut out the messages, to make separate cards or slips.

Activity

This is an activity for up to eight children. Explain about the characters in the game. Tell the children that they are going to try to deliver some messages, changing the way they speak and act according to the character they pretend to be talking to. Shuffle the character cards, and place them in a pile face down. The adult keeps the message cards. The children stand or sit in a circle, and you tell them the first message. It is a good idea for everyone to practise saying it so that they can remember it when it is their turn. Choose a child to be the first messenger. The messenger takes the top character card without letting anyone see it. They turn to the child on their left, pretending that the child is the character on the card, and deliver the message. The group has to guess which character it is. The child who has received the message becomes the next messenger, and takes the next card from the pile. Several children should have a go at the same message, but if there are seven or eight players you may want to change the message when you are half way round the circle.

Extension

Make a set of different characters, which could be linked to topic work.

USING SPEECH EFFECTIVELY

Stage I

Stage II

Stage III

Stage IV

Circle Time

Hall/PE

Literacy

Numeracy

Drama

Small Group

Art

Humanities

Science

Design Technology

PHSE

Food Technology

Goatherds

Aim
To be able to project the voice a specific distance, and in a specific direction.

Equipment

List of goats' names from Teaching Resources (page 273).

Preparation

Prepare a copy of the list of goats' names for yourself.

Activity

You might like to introduce this activity by telling the children how goatherds in mountain areas (such as the Tyrol) communicate with each other over large distances. They can use yodelling, but the children are only going to use ordinary voices! Four children are going to be positioned, one in each corner of the hall, as far away as possible from the child is who is doing the speaking (the goatherd). The goatherd calls out to each of the four children in turn, facing towards them and naming a goat that he has lost. The purpose of using made-up names is that the listeners cannot use context to make up for poor audibility. The goatherd uses the same sentence each time: 'I've lost … Have you seen him/her?' The adult supplies the name each time from the list. The child to whom the goatherd is calling must reply, repeating the goat's name. Have they got it right?

Example

Goatherd: I've lost Bumble. Have you seen him?
Listener: Bumble.

Tip

The goatherds may tend to shout. If a child has played the goatherd and been successful in conveying his message, but shouted, see if he can do it again by using a raised speaking voice instead of a shout.

Stage I

Stage II

Stage III

Stage IV

Circle Time

Hall/PE

Literacy

Numeracy

Drama

Small Group

Art

Humanities

Science

Design Technology

PHSE

Food Technology

USING SPEECH EFFECTIVELY

Direction-Finder

Aim

To be able to look at the audience during the reading of short pieces of text.

Equipment

None.

Preparation

'Write out two-line instructions on individual cards as suggested in the examples below. You may wish to include the instructions on when to make eye contact, as in the examples, or you may leave the children to work it out for themselves.

Activity

Explain that people are going to take turns to read out a two-part instruction or question. The reader stands in front of the class or group, which is lined up in a semi-circle. It is essential that the reader can see every one's face clearly. The reader is given a message card, and can take a look at it to grasp the gist. They then decide to which child in the group they will address the message. They read out the first line of the message, and make eye contact with the intended recipient. They then read out the second part of the instruction or question, and look again at the other child.
The recipient must wait until both parts of the message have been given, and then respond by carrying out the instruction, or by answering the question.

Examples

'I'm going to ask you a question. (Make eye contact) What letter does your first name begin with?' (Look again.)
'Get ready to do something for me. (Make eye contact). Put both your hands on your head.' (Look again.)

Catch a Name

Aim

To be able to invent and correct spoonerisms, by swapping initial sounds – for example, 'Lenny Henry' becomes 'Henny Lenry'.

Equipment

A bean-bag.
A list of names (see examples below).

Activity

Divide the group into two teams. They should stand in two separate lines, facing each other. Give the bean-bag to the first child in the group and show them the first name. They have to turn it into a spoonerism, and call it out to the opposite team. They then throw the bean-bag to someone in the opposite team, who has to try to repeat the correct version of the name. If they are right, they earn a point for their team, and you tell them the next name. Continue until everyone has had a turn.

Example

Harry Potter	Julius Caesar
William Shakespeare	David Beckham
Bart Simpson	Will Young
Mr Bean	Peter Rabbit
Prince Charles	Winnie the Pooh
Tom and Jerry	Frank Bruno
Wallace and Grommit	Roald Dahl
Walt Disney	Homer Simpson
John Lennon	Frodo Baggins
Lord Nelson	Tony Blair
Guy Fawkes	Jonny Wilkinson
Florence Nightingale	Rolf Harris

Stage I

Stage II

Stage III

Stage IV

Circle Time

Hall/PE

Literacy

Numeracy

Drama

Small Group

Art

Humanities

Science

Design Technology

PHSE

Food Technology

USING SPEECH EFFECTIVELY

Stage I

Stage II

Stage III

Stage IV

Circle Time

Hall/PE

Literacy

Numeracy

Drama

Small Group

Art

Humanities

Science

Design Technology

PHSE

Food Technology

Ring the Changes

Aim
To be able to use intonation to change meaning, and to understand the words 'intonation', 'stress' and 'emphasise'.

Equipment

'Ring the Changes' sentences from Teaching Resources (page 274).

Preparation

Copy the sentences, and cut them out into individual slips.

Activity

Distribute the slips, one to each child. In turns the children stand up and speak their sentence, using as much gesture, emphasis, intonation and general dramatisation as they can to enhance the meaning. Then hands up – who can think of a different way of saying that sentence to change the meaning slightly? How many different ways of saying it can they think of? Discuss how the meanings can change. Once the children have got the idea, divide them into teams, and see which team can reach the biggest total of variations.

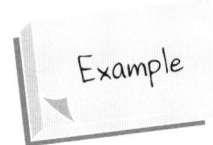

Example

Where have I put my blue jumper this time?
Where have I put my blue jumper **this** time?
Where **have** I put my blue jumper this time?
Where have I put my **blue** jumper this time?
Where have I put my blue **jumper** this time?

USING SPEECH EFFECTIVELY

Correct Me!

Aim
To be able to recognise a pronunciation error and correct it.

Equipment

'Correct Me!' sentences (page 275) and Raceboard (page 198) from Teaching Resources.
Counters and die.

Preparation

Cut the sentences into cards.

Activity

The first child throws the die, and moves the number of spaces indicated. If they land on a star, you take the first card, and read it exactly as it is written. If the child can identify which word has an error, they move forward one space. If they can correct the error, they move forward one more space. If they can do neither, they stay in the same place. You can make your own rules regarding the smiley and sad faces on the Raceboard. You can make an additional set of error sentences.

Stage I

Stage II

Stage III

Stage IV

Circle Time

Hall/PE

Literacy

Numeracy

Drama

Small Group

Art

Humanities

Science

Design Technology

PHSE

Food Technology

Stage I

Stage II

Stage III

Stage IV

Circle Time

Hall/PE

Literacy

Numeracy

Drama

Small Group

Art

Humanities

Science

Design Technology

PHSE

Food Technology

USING SPEECH EFFECTIVELY

Wordpix

Aim
To be able to pronounce words with several syllables clearly.

Equipment

'Wordpix' examples and sample word list from Teaching Resources (pages 276–277).

Preparation

Choose a maximum of five words for a session. The word list supplied is taken from the Key Stage 2 Science curriculum but you may wish to include or substitute other words. Break the words down into single or double syllables. This should be displayed in one of the following ways: single syllables are written inside a cartoon figure, or represented by a single capital letter; some syllables and double syllables can be illustrated by a picture.

Activity

Tell the children you are all going to learn how to say some hard new words. You have invented a really easy way to do this. First say the new word. Then put up the first cartoon figure, letter or picture. Everyone says it. Put up the next part, everyone says it. Gradually combine the separate parts until the whole word can be said.

USING SPEECH EFFECTIVELY

Stage I

Stage II

Stage III

Stage IV

Circle Time

Hall/PE

Literacy

Numeracy

Drama

Small Group

Art

Humanities

Science

Design Technology

PHSE

Food Technology

Tangled Tongues

Aim

To be able to pronounce clearly and accurately the words in a tongue twister.

Equipment

'Tangled Tongues' tongue-twisters from Teaching Resources (page 278).
A stopwatch.

Preparation

Copy and cut out the tongue-twisters, enough for each child to have one.

Activity

Tell the children that they are going to practise saying some quite complicated tongue-twisters, getting faster and faster. This is the sort of thing that actors, film stars and newsreaders have to do. Match the difficulty of the tongue-twisters to the ability of the children as far as possible. Let the children draw lots for who will go first, and give the child a tongue-twister. Let them read it silently, and you might go through it aloud together, or with the whole group. Then start the stopwatch, and say 'Go!' The child reads the tongue-twister as slowly as necessary, in order to pronounce each word correctly. When they finish, stop the watch, tell them how long they took, and note the time down. That child will have another turn later, either the same day or on another occasion, and see if they can beat their time.

Examples

Sister Susie's sewing socks for sailors. Where are the sailors' socks Sister Susie sewed?
Which switch is the switch Miss for Ipswich? It's the Ipswich switch which I require.

Stage I
Stage II
Stage III
Stage IV
Circle Time
Hall/PE
Literacy
Numeracy
Drama
Small Group
Art
Humanities
Science
Design Technology
PHSE
Food Technology

USING SPEECH EFFECTIVELY

Done to a T

Aim
To be able to pronounce words with single or double 't' in the middle.

Equipment

'Done to a T' lists of half-words from Teaching Resources (page 279).

Preparation

Copy the two lists of half-words.

Activity

Divide the children into two teams, with pairs standing opposite each other. The purpose of the game is to pronounce the words on the lists correctly, sounding the medial 't'. You may have to demonstrate! Some of the children in the class will already pronounce these words correctly quite naturally. Others substitute a glottal stop for the medial 't' – for example, 'bu – er' for 'butter'. The half-words are read out alternately by members of the two teams, fairly fast, so that each pair produces the whole word or phrase between them. The adult or adults adjudicate – when anybody misses out the 't' sound, he and his opposite number are out and sit down. This first well-known tongue-twister is just for practice: (Betty – Botter, bought some – batter, but she said – my batter's bitter.)

Example

Child 1: Pitter- Child 2: -patter. Child 3: Helter- Child 4: -skelter. Child 5: Water- Child 6: -beetle. Child 7: Nitty- Child 8: -gritty.

Tips

Substituting a glottal stop for medial 't' is a very widespread dialect form, and you are not going to change it with this activity! However, teachers sometimes find that the mispronunciation of these words leads to spelling errors, and this game aims to highlight where a 't' *should* be, even if it is not normally there!

USING SPEECH EFFECTIVELY

Make a Play

Aim
To be able to convert text into dialogue.

Equipment

'Make a Play' texts from Teaching Resources (page 280).

Preparation

Select a text. Each text includes six characters presented in pairs. This means that the number of characters can be adjusted according to the size of the group.

Activity

This activity is suitable for a group of up to six children. Explain that you are going to make a short play together. (You may need to make sure that everyone understands what a play is.) Read through the text once, and find out if the children have understood the main theme. Ask how many characters they think there are, and make a note on the whiteboard or scrap paper. Each child is then assigned a character. The first pair of characters stands up. Read the text to them, then allow them the opportunity to turn the appropriate parts into dialogue. Continue in this way until everyone has had a turn. You can then go through the whole text again, with each character contributing a speaking part.

Extension

The text could be transformed into a drama. and be performed. Children could write the spoken parts in Literacy, paying attention to correct punctuation.

| Stage I |
| Stage II |
| Stage III |
| **Stage IV** |
| Circle Time |
| Hall/PE |
| Literacy |
| Numeracy |
| **Drama** |
| Small Group |
| Art |
| Humanities |
| Science |
| Design Technology |
| PHSE |
| Food Technology |

Stage I

Stage II

Stage III

Stage IV

Circle Time

Hall/PE

Literacy

Numeracy

Drama

Small Group

Art

Humanities

Science

Design Technology

PHSE

Food Technology

USING SPEECH EFFECTIVELY

Choose Your Words!

Aim
To be able to use precise and effective vocabulary, and to avoid empty words or phrases such as 'I mean', 'you know', 'stuff' and 'like'.

Equipment

'Choose Your Words!' list of the 'banned' words and expressions from Teaching Resources (page 281), with boxes beside each one in which a tick or cross can be placed for scoring.

Preparation

Photocopy the score sheets, and give one to each child.

Activity

Explain that everyone is going to have a turn at giving a short speech or lecture. They are to try to do it without using any of the 'banned' words and phrases. The rest of the group will be listening, and keeping score by putting a mark in the appropriate box every time they hear a banned word. Speakers will start off with 10 points, and at the end one point is deducted for every banned word identified. The public speaker award goes to the child who retains the most points. You can give the speakers any topics you want – for example: how to make a sponge cake; what they did at the weekend; the theme of a film or television programme; their favourite pastime, and why they enjoy it.

Tip

If the score-keeping proves difficult, allocate certain children to listen for just one of the banned words or phrases. They can combine their scores at the end of each speech.

Extension

Tape some extracts of interviews heard on radio or television. (Choose with care!) Can the children spot the speakers using any 'empty' words?

USING SPEECH EFFECTIVELY

Messengers (2)

Stage I

Stage II

Stage III

Stage IV

Circle Time

Hall/PE

Literacy

Numeracy

Drama

Small Group

Art

Humanities

Science

Design Technology

PHSE

Food Technology

Aim

To be able to convey a question or instruction in a manner appropriate to the listener, using appropriate words.

Equipment

'Messengers (2)' names of 'listeners' and list of 'messages' from Teaching Resources (page 282).

Preparation

Make at least four copies of each listener card. Make a copy of the list of messages.

Activity

This is an activity for a group of not more than 10 children. This is played in the same way as 'Messengers (1)' but is more difficult because the children are expected to change the *wording* of the message as well as the manner of speaking. Explain about the characters in the game. Tell the children that they are going to try to deliver some messages, changing the words they use, and the way they speak and act, according to the character they are talking to. Shuffle the character cards, and place them in a pile face down. The adult keeps the message cards, and reads out a message. The first child takes the top character card without letting anyone see it. They turn to the child on their left, pretending that the child is the character on the card. They must attempt to word the message in such a way that the listener will understand, and not be upset, confused or offended by it. Can the group guess to whom they are speaking?

USING SPEECH EFFECTIVELY

Stage I

Stage II

Stage III

Stage IV

Circle Time

Hall/PE

Literacy

Numeracy

Drama

Small Group

Art

Humanities

Science

Design Technology

PHSE

Food Technology

Story Crowd

Aim
To be able to adopt a speaking style to match a specific character.

Equipment

'Story Crowd' character cards, character list and messages from Teaching Resources (page 283).

Preparation

Everyone in the group will need a character card. The messages can be enlarged or highlighted as necessary.

Activity

Go through the character cards to familiarise the children with them. Place the character cards face down on the table. Each child takes one without showing it to anyone else. Make sure everyone knows their character. Pin the message to the whiteboard, and read it out to everyone. Allow time to practise memorising and repeating the message. Pin up the character list. The first child says their message in the manner of their character. Ask the rest of the group which character they think it is. When you have found the correct character, tick it off the character list, and the person who identified the character says the message in the manner of their character. Continue until everyone has had a turn.

USING SPEECH EFFECTIVELY

Stage I

Stage II

Stage III

Stage IV

Circle Time

Hall/PE

Literacy

Numeracy

Drama

Small Group

Art

Humanities

Science

Design Technology

PHSE

Food Technology

Poetry Challenge

Aim
To be able to learn and recite a poem.

Equipment

Poetry books from class or school.

Activity

Ask the children if they know any poems off by heart. If anyone does, they may like to recite it. Then set the challenge, which is to learn a poem, or part of a poem, in a given time. Read a selection of short poems to the group, and take a vote on the most popular. When you have made a choice, ask each member of the group how much of the poem they think they can learn, in a set time decided on by you. Make a note of the responses. You will then need to recite the poem again, explaining the meaning of any unfamiliar words, and drawing attention to the rhythm, rhyme and other features which may help with memorising. It would be a good idea to give each member of the group a copy of their challenge – that is, the amount they think they can learn. At the end of the agreed time, each member of the group has the opportunity to recite their 'piece' in front of the rest. Marks may be given for accuracy, clarity and expression.

Tip

The time allowed can be anything from a few hours to several days, depending on the length of the poem and timetable restrictions.

Stage I

Stage II

Stage III

Stage IV

Circle Time

Hall/PE

Literacy

Numeracy

Drama

Small Group

Art

Humanities

Science

Design Technology

PHSE

Food Technology

USING SPEECH EFFECTIVELY

Pop Speaker

Aim
To be able to deliver a short text with appropriate speed, volume and intonation, while looking at the audience from time to time.

Equipment

Short pieces of text, fiction or non-fiction, of not more than seven or eight lines.

Preparation

For this activity, the preparation is done by the children taking part. Each child must choose a piece of text, and either write it out or prepare it on the computer. The children can work out for themselves how to indicate the points at which they will pause and look up at their audience. This will probably be at the end of every two or three sentences, depending on sentence length. (Practised speakers read a sentence or so ahead, and deliver this from memory before looking back at the text.) The children also need to work out how to find their place again when they have raised their eyes from the text.

Activity

Choose a confident child to go first. They take their place in front of the group, deliver their speech and receive a round of applause. Move on to the next speaker.

Extension

If the children in the group are confident enough, and of a fairly consistent ability level, you can turn this into a 'Pop Speaker' contest on the lines of 'Pop Idol'. Each child will either start with 10 points and the audience will deduct points for faulty delivery, or will start with nil points and be awarded up to 10. Who emerges as the Pop Speaker?

Understanding & Using Spoken Language
ACTIVITY RESOURCES

TEACHING RESOURCES

Resources

Stage I

Active
Listening &
Memory

Harriet's Hats

Monday

Tuesday

Wednesday

Thursday

Friday

Saturday

Sunday

Waiter!

Stage I

Active Listening & Memory

Give it a Name

1 Once upon a time there was a princess who was very pretty, very rich and very bad-tempered. She didn't have any friends because she was always so grumpy to the little princes and princesses her parents invited round. One day she was in her beautiful garden, sulking as usual, and saying how bored she was. Suddenly she heard a rustling in the bushes, and a tiny little man – no taller than her knee – appeared.

2 Dan and his mum were shopping in the supermarket. Mum was taking ages to choose a box of washing powder. Dan noticed that there were some cool CDs on the next shelf, so he went to have a look at them. He soon found one he wanted, so he caught up with his mum, in her green coat, to ask her for the money to buy one. Imagine the shock he had when she turned around, and she was not his mum!

3 Milly was spending the day at her auntie's house. It was pouring with rain so she couldn't play outside, and there was nothing good on the television. Auntie Beth was busy working at her computer, and Milly was bored. Auntie Beth said, 'Go upstairs and look in the big box on the landing – there are some dressing-up clothes you might like.' Milly went up and opened the box. On the top were a couple of jumpers and a long black skirt. She rummaged a bit deeper, and pulled out a purple hat with a wide brim. Then she found a little bag with sparkly sequins sewn all over the outside. She opened the bag, and a silver coin fell out.

4 Louise was feeling very nervous. Any minute now it would be her turn to go on. Her costume felt tight, her mouth was dry. She was sure she would forget the words. The Year 4 dance routine ended with a lot of clapping. Louise took a deep breath and stepped onto the stage.

5 The two boys set off up the mountain. The sun was shining and the sky was a clear deep blue. They followed the path as it became steep and winding. As they got higher the wind began to blow, and dark clouds started to build up. The clouds got bigger and bigger, and suddenly the boys realised that they were surrounded by a thick grey mist. In front of them the path divided in two. They could no longer see the village below them, or the top of the mountain above.

Character Sketch

Stage II

Active
Listening &
Memory

1 Molly the witch has long black hair, a tall black hat, and a red dress.

2 Sam the sailor has a patch over one eye. His shirt is blue and white stripes, and he has a beard.

3 Mrs Fudge wears glasses. Her hair is short and curly, and she is rather fat.

4 Kyle is tall and thin. He has spiky hair and sticking out ears.

5 Dr Fix is bald. He carries a black bag, and wears a bright green tie.

6 Farmer Jim wears a hat, a big coat and wellington boots. He smokes a pipe.

7 Ben is only three. He has curly blonde hair and carries his teddy wherever he goes.

8 Old Miss Pink walks with a walking stick. She has short white hair and wears glasses.

9 Mr Ross has ginger hair and a beard. He is carrying his garden fork and a watering can.

10 Gus plays in a band. He has long hair and he is playing his guitar.

11 Kelly is eight. She has brown hair in plaits and always wears trousers.

12 Ricky Finn is a painter. He is carrying a ladder and a big tin of paint.

What were they Doing?

1 Jemma badly needed a new dress for the party. She stood and looked in the shop window for ages. There were such beautiful things in it! There was a long red dress with frilly sleeves, and a pretty blue one with stars on it. Jemma wondered if she would have enough money for either of them, as she had spent a lot on her expensive holiday abroad recently. She looked at her watch, and realised it was nearly time for the bus. 'I'll just have to make up my mind', she thought, and pushed open the door.

(Question: What was Jemma doing? Answer: Shopping for a party dress.)

2 Jamilla began to wonder if the time for the actual performance would ever come. They had been through the whole thing four times already. 'Here we go again', she thought, as Mrs Swan the teacher lined up the children . 'Right children', said Mrs Swan, 'Now I want to hear every word clearly, and mind you remember that top note.' Mrs Swan played a loud chord on the piano, and the song began. It went quite well that time. 'Your turn now, Jamilla', said Mrs Swan. 'Come out to the front with your recorder.' Jamilla felt a little nervous, but she got through her piece without a mistake. 'Should be all right tomorrow', she thought.

(Question: What were the children doing? Answer: Rehearsing for an assembly, show or a concert.)

3 Simon really hated this job. The puppy was a champion wriggler, and in the struggle you usually got soaked. Sometimes Topsy nipped your fingers, too. 'She really must be done today', Dad said, 'She's muddy and smelly. And its your turn, Simon.' With a sigh, Simon began to collect the things he needed – the big bowl, the dog shampoo, a brush, and a towel. He filled the bowl with warm water to make it a bit nicer. Then he went to fetch the puppy, but of course she had disappeared – she knew what was going to happen. Simon thought he knew where to look, and he went quietly out to the garden shed. Sure enough, there was Topsy, looking very unhappy, with her tail between her legs.

(Question: What was Simon going to do? Answer: Bath the dog.)

What were they Doing? *(continued)*

Stage II

Active
Listening &
Memory

4 It was the day of the match, and Nathan felt quite sick with excitement.
The goalkeeper's job was so important and he just hoped he wouldn't let
everybody down. He hunted out his team shirt, his shorts, boots and
socks. 'Hurry up', Dad called from downstairs, 'Its only half an hour to the
kick-off.' Nathan clattered down the stairs, dropping things and picking
them up again on his way. 'Are you going to stay and watch the match,
Dad?', he asked. 'I certainly am', Dad said, 'And I'm bringing the video
camera too, so I can record the Save of the Century.' Nathan said goodbye
to his Mum. 'Good luck', she said, 'I'll be thinking of you all afternoon.'

(Question: What is Nathan going to do? Answer: Play as goalkeeper in
the football match.)

Word Alert (1)

1 The waves *crashed* onto the beach. Zad *hoisted* his surf-board onto his shoulder and *sprinted* towards the sea. He *waded* through the shallow water. Then he *climbed* onto the board and *paddled* it out to where the really big breakers were *gathering*. (7 points)

2 There were four eggs in the nest. A crack *appeared* in one of the eggs. After a while the egg *split* open and a tiny bird *staggered* out. At first it *wobbled* and *lurched* around the nest, *bumping* into the other eggs. Gradually it *opened* its eyes and *squinted* in the sunlight. Then it cautiously *spread* its damp wings and *opened* its beak to *take* its first meal. (11 points)

3 The lioness *dozed* in the sun. Around her the four cubs *played* with each other. Suddenly her nose *twitched* and her eyes *flew* open. She *jumped* to her feet and *padded* slowly out of the clearing. Then she *crouched* down and *watched* her prey. After a minute she *pounced*. (9 points)

4 Anna was bored. She *wandered* into the garden and *perched* on the swing. It was a hot day and bees *buzzed* among the flowers. High above, a plane *droned* across the sky. Where was everyone? She *swung* gently, *scuffing* the ground with her feet. What was that? Immediately Anna *leapt* off the swing and *ran* over to the fence. (8 points)

5 There was a black horse in the field. He was *grazing* peacefully, until the train *roared* by. Then he *snorted* loudly, *kicked* his heels and *galloped* madly round the field. He *skidded* to a stop at the gate and *reared* up on his hind legs. (7 points)

6 The sky was dark and thunder *rumbled* in the distance. Large drops of rain *plopped* noisily onto the roof. The thunder got louder and lightning *flashed* across the sky, *lighting* up the horizon. A huge clap of thunder *ripped* through the air. Now hail stones *pelted* down and water *gushed* down the street. The wind *roared* in the trees, the clouds *scudded* across the sky. It was a terrible night to be out *riding* a bike. (10 points)

Speechmark Ⓟ

Word Alert (1) *(continued)*

7 It was Kim's birthday. She *jumped* out of bed and *ran* downstairs. There was a pile of presents and cards on the kitchen table. Kim *gazed* longingly at them and *wished* everyone would get up. The biggest present was a funny shape, and Kim *prodded* it. Then she *heard* a noise from upstairs. It was her brother Joe, *clambering* down off the top bunk. He *appeared* at the top of the stairs, *clutching* his favourite teddy. (9 points)

8 The curtain was *raised* slowly as the music *boomed* out. Max *walked* bravely onto the stage. He *stared* straight at the audience as he *spoke*. Soon he was *joined* by the other actors. Max *flung* his arms wide and *shouted* his final lines to the audience. They *applauded* loudly, *clapping* their hands and *stamping* their feet. (11 points)

9 Mick and Josh *skidded* to a halt. They had just *zoomed* down the hill on their skateboards. They *panted* as they *kicked* the boards to one side and *leant* against the fence. Mick *reached* in his pocket and *pulled* out a packet of gum. He *offered* it to Josh, who *took* it and *ripped* off the paper. (10 points)

10 Kali *loved* cooking. She was *helping* her mum bake a special cake for her auntie. Mum *measured* the ingredients carefully, and *spooned* the flour into the mixture. Kali *beat* the butter and sugar together. Then they *poured* the mixture into a cake tin and *placed* it in the middle of the oven. (7 points)

Stage II

Active Listening & Memory

Whose Birthday?

You might be old and you might be grey,
But you're really special in every way.
Grandmother

You're so cool and tall,
And you always kick the ball.
Elder Brother

You care for us, you're really great,
And you only look about twenty-eight.
Mum

You go to work and earn the money,
You take out the rubbish and are nice to mummy.
Dad

You like dollies, you dress in pink,
You're younger than me, but you're OK I think.
Younger Sister

You're my mummy's sister and you live quite far away.
We really want to see you – have a lovely day.
Aunt

Greetings, daddy's brother, on your very special day.
Have a brilliant outing and make sure the others pay!
Uncle

Long, long ago, when you were a boy,
A box of tin soldiers was a wonderful toy.
Grandfather

Commercials

Stage II

Active
Listening &
Memory

1 It's the new superfast, safe and comfortable way to travel. It's sleek and streamlined, quiet and smooth. It corners without you noticing it, and you won't even see your glass shake. London to Manchester in two hours 10 minutes, this is the transport of the future: the new Supatrain!

2 It's the smallest yet! It fits in your inside pocket, or in a purse or wallet and weighs almost nothing. More functions than ever before, and an almost country-wide cover. Can't be used if stolen. Use it for the internet as well as for calling your mates or texting. The Mini-talk is the latest in mobile phones.

3 So quiet you can hardly hear it, even if you're standing right next to it. So quick the longest programme only takes 20 minutes. Guaranteed to give you 10 years of uninterrupted service. The tumble programme means you'll hardly ever have to iron. This is the machine for anyone who wants whiter whites and softer woollens – the Whitewater Rapids Washing Machine.

4 The professionals are using it! It's tiny, lightweight and fully automatic. It will give you good results indoors, outdoors, in shady or full sun conditions. You want to capture that bird on the distant tree, or that butterfly in close-up on the flower? Self-setting focus and automatic flash control mean you don't have to worry – just point and shoot. This is the camera for everyone!

5 Ultra-light yet robust, you can take this with you on the train, or fold it up and take it in the car. Sturdy enough for all surfaces and road conditions. It comes with metallic paint in a wide range of colours. Hand grips in the latest non-slip material. The 20 gears mean easy riding up any gradient. You'll be the envy of your friends with the Porta-genie mountain bike.

6 You can pick it up with one hand, and with a quick shake of the wrist it folds down flat. Three wheel design means it will travel easily both on roads and over rough ground. Strong enough to carry up to 20 kilos, and with secure braking system. Under-seat basket allows for ample shopping space. Cover for rainy days included, and a special hook for attaching baby's favourite toy. This is the season's best buggy buy.

Stop Thief!

1 This incident took place *last Thursday*, at about *two in the afternoon*. Three boys were passing the *jeweller's shop, Diamonds Forever*, when they noticed a man running out of the front door, stuffing something into his pocket. He was *short and dark*, and was wearing a *black leather jacket and white trainers*. He jumped into a waiting car, a *green Ford Cortina*, *registration number R 929 ABC*, which made off at high speed round the corner. One of the boys who witnessed the robbery was *very tall and thin, with gingery hair*. If anyone can help, please contact the police.

(Ask the children or groups to look out for: the day; the time of the day; the kind of shop; the name of the shop; the appearance of the thief; the make and colour of the getaway car; the car's registration number, and the appearance of one of the witnesses.)

2 A snatch-and-run raid took place *yesterday* at *Bingo's Bank* in *(any nearby town)*. Two men, wearing black balaclavas, black jumpers and black jeans held up the staff at the bank at about *10 in the morning*. The bank was full of customers at the time. One of the bank staff remembers that she was serving an *Indian lady*, who was *wearing a beautiful sari*. The thief escaped from the bank and zoomed off on a *Harley Davidson motorbike*. He dropped a *small blue notebook* on the pavement outside the bank.

(Ask the children or groups to listen out for: the day; the name of the bank; the name of the town; the clothes the thief was wearing; the time of day; the appearance of one of the bank customers; how the thief drove off and what he dropped which might form a clue.)

3 An unusual robbery took place on *April 2nd*, just before closing time, at *5.25 pm*. The shop targeted was *a pet shop*, called *Cats and Dogs*. The thief made off with a *box of maggots,* which the shop owner kept for fishing trips. Police think that the robber mistook the box for one containing a *rare and valuable lizard*. The man ran away carrying the box, and although one or two bystanders tried to stop him, he made his escape and jumped on a *Number nine bus*. The man was wearing a distinctive *red jumpsuit*. One gentleman who tried to tackle him was an *elderly man with a beard*, who attempted to stop him with his walking stick.

(Ask the children or groups to listen out for: the date; the time of the robbery; the type of shop; the name of the shop what was stolen; what the police thought the robber meant to steal; the number of the bus and the appearance of the witness.)

Speechmark **P**
Understanding & Using Spoken Language © C Delamain & J Spring 2004

Poetry Please

It runs like a silver ribbon,
Whispering over the weeds.
The willows bend over its ripples,
As it winds between the reeds. (stream or river)

This creature cannot make you laugh,
Whistle, dance or sing,
And he ain't much to look at,
And he don't make anything.
And in amongst his prickles
There's fleas and bugs and that,
But there ain't no need for cars to leave him
Squashed. And dead. And flat. (hedgehog)

I am a little animal,
Sitting in me hutch;
I like to sit up this end,
I don't care for that end, much.
I wash me shiny whiskers,
And chomp me little teef,
And eat a bit of carrot,
And another lettuce leaf. (rabbit)

Her skirt was brightest crimson,
And black her steeple hat;
Her broomstick lay beside her,
I'm positive of that.
Her chin was sharp and pointed,
Her eyes were – I don't know –
For, when she turned towards me
I thought it best – to go! (witch)

Poetry Please *(continued)*

Their tails are long,
Their faces small,
They haven't any chins at all;
Their ears are pink,
Their teeth are white;
They run about the house at night.
They nibble things they shouldn't touch,
And no one seems to like them much.   (mice)

With their feet in the earth,
And their heads in the sky,
They stand and watch
The clouds go by.
When the dusk sends quickly
The birds to rest,
They shelter them safely,
Tucked in a nest.   (trees)

Standing firm upon the rocks
In the tossing foam,
Its light shines out to help me
Steer my vessel home.   (lighthouse)

Underneath the water-weeds,
Small and black, I wriggle,
And life is most surprising!
Wiggle! Waggle! Wiggle!
There's every now and then a most
Exciting change in me;
I wonder, wiggle! waggle!
What I *shall* turn out to be!   (tadpole)

Poetry Please *(continued)*

A green eye – and a red – in the dark;
Thunder – smoke – and a spark;
It is there – it is here – flashed by.
Whither will this wild thing fly?
It is rushing, tearing through the night,
Rending her gloom in its flight.   (steam train)

This stuff has no taste at all,
This stuff has no smell;
This stuff's in the waterfall,
In pump, and tap, and well.
This stuff's everywhere about,
This stuff's in the rain;
In the bath, the pond, and out
At sea, it's there again.   (water)

Stage III

Active
Listening &
Memory

Word Alert (2)

1 They stepped outside into the *freezing* morning. The wind blew *icy* gusts in their faces. The whole valley was hidden under a *deep* blanket of snow. Overhead, *heavy grey* clouds hung and already *feathery* snowflakes were beginning to fall. (6 points)

2 The *stone* house at the end of the track had been empty for years. Ivy clung to its *crumbling* walls and you could see bats through the *cracked* window panes. The *overgrown* garden was full of nettles and brambles and birds had nested in the *rotting* thatch. If you looked through the *broken* window, you could see a *huge rusty* kettle on the *dusty* table. (9 points)

3 Nina was sitting on the *wooden* bench in the garden. Her *blue* pen lay on the table by the *open* Maths book. It was a *hot* day and she couldn't do the *hard* Maths homework. She gazed up into the *deep blue* sky. High up, she could see the *silver* wings of a plane. She wished she was up there, on her way to an *amazing* holiday. (9 points)

4 Snuffles was a *small black* pony with a *white* star on his nose. Sasha loved to stroke his *silky* mane when he came over to the gate to get a piece of *crunchy* apple from her hand. He belonged to *scary* Miss Stirrup at the riding stables. Miss Stirrup wore *corduroy* trousers and *green* boots and had a *croaky* voice. (9 points)

5 Max looked at the *long, steep* hill ahead. It was going to take ages to climb to the top, especially carrying the *heavy* bag of fishing tackle. Still, it would be worth it once he was sitting on the *cool* river bank, watching the *rippling* water, dreaming of a *fat* trout. He started trudging forwards, one *weary* step after another. When he reached the top he was panting and his face was *red,* but he could see the *silvery* river in the distance. (9 points)

6 It was a *hot* Saturday afternoon and Jamilla and Sandy were walking through the *busy* shopping mall. They were looking for a present for Sandy's mum. 'It's got to be really *special,* 'cos she's going to be 40,' said Sandy. They looked in the window of a shop selling china. There was a *huge glass* vase, with *gleaming* pebbles in the bottom. Sandy sighed. It was much too *expensive.* Then Jamilla nudged her and pointed to a *little* table just inside the shop. On it stood a *beautiful blue* jug. (10 points)

Speechmark Ⓟ
Understanding & Using Spoken Language © C Delamain & J Spring 2004

Word Alert (2) *(continued)*

Stage III

Active Listening & Memory

7 Georgie was *nervous*. The race started in five minutes. She stood at the edge of the *glittering* pool, watching the *flat* surface of the water. The other contestants were lining up, with *determined* faces, holding their *fluffy* towels. Georgie took her place and waited. In a few minutes she would plunge into the *deep cool* water and do her best, cutting through the foam with *deep* strokes. (8 points)

8 It was *dark* in the forest. Looking up, Carly could see *little* patches of *blue* sky through the *tall* trees. Under her feet was a blanket of *crunchy* leaves and *crackling* twigs. She walked forwards and then she heard a sound. It came from high in the *twisted* branches of an oak tree. Looking up she saw two *red* squirrels running along the *smooth* branches. They had *bright* eyes and *bushy* tails. (11 points)

Stage III

Active
Listening &
Memory

Get Organised!

1   The blue group are going to finish their stories. They will need their
Literacy books and a pencil. The red group are going to do Art. You need
your Art overall, paints, brushes and water. The yellow group are going to
the hall to practise their PE display. Take the bean-bags and hoops and
two balls. The green group are practising measuring, using rulers, metre
sticks and a tape-measure.

2   The red group are going to make a model. You need glue, scissors, an
egg box and pipe-cleaners. Green group need to finish your cards. You
can decorate them with stars, buttons or ribbons. Blue group will be
working with Mrs Smith in the library. Take your reading book, a pencil
and a piece of paper. Yellow group are carrying on with the magnets
investigation. You need paper-clips, a magnet, a rubber, a wooden spoon
and a metal spoon.

3   Green group – it's time for shared reading. Get your books and sit at the
table by the window. Red group – you need to finish your History work.
You will need tracing paper, a pencil and a sheet of plain white paper.
Yellow group take your History folders to the Library and don't forget you
will need colouring pencils. Blue group will be watching the Science
video. You need to make some notes in your jotter and highlight the
names of different materials.

4   Yellow group: you are going to work on capacity with Miss Smith. You
will need aprons, a jug each and two small beakers. Blue group: you will
need your swimming kit ready for after break, and you will be making
the front cover for your story book. You can use felt-tip pens and gel
pens. Green group are working on symmetry. Make sure you have a
mirror, paper, a pencil and a ruler. Red group: it's your turn to practise for
sports day. Put on your PE kit and take a bottle of water each.

Get Organised! *(continued)*

Stage III

Active
Listening &
Memory

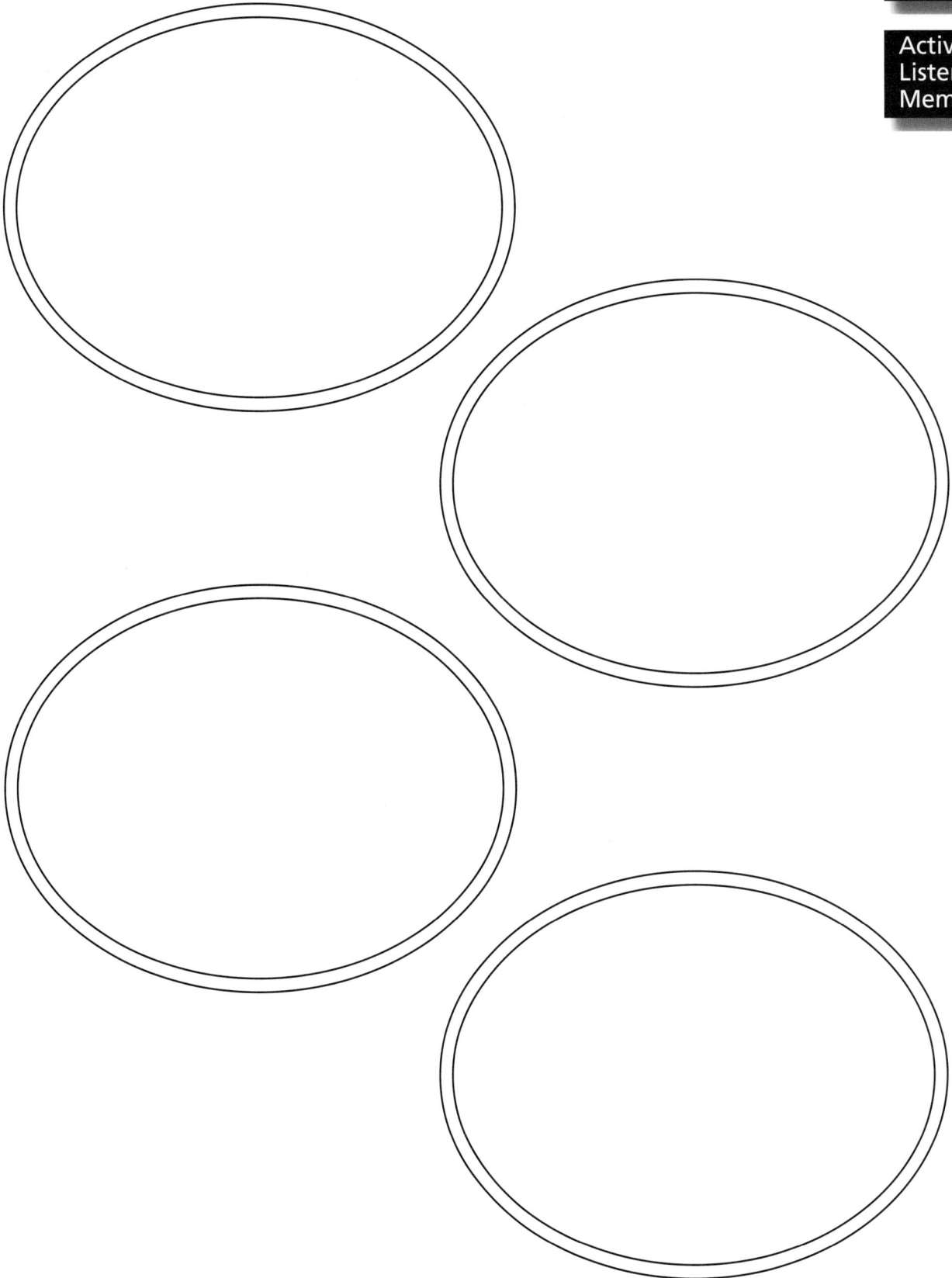

Calendar

1 Don't forget Nan's birthday on the fourth.

2 And the day after that it's swimming.

3 I've asked your cousins over on the first Saturday.

4 We've got to go to the dentist on the 17th.

5 I hope I can get tickets for the concert the Saturday after the dentist's.

6 And on that Sunday we are going to see your uncle.

7 Dan's birthday is on the 20th, but he's having his party on the following Saturday.

8 Remember to mark in gym club every Monday.

9 The new washing machine should be delivered on Tuesday 18th.

10 A week later, the man is coming to mend the roof.

Calendar *(continued)*

Stage III

Active Listening & Memory

Sun	Mon	Tue	Wed	Thu	Fri	Sat
			1	2	3	4
5	6	7	8	9	10	11
12	13	14	15	16	17	18
19	20	21	22	23	24	25
26	27	28	29	30	31	

Ask Me a Question

1 When Joe got home the house was quiet. This was odd, because she was usually home before him. He flopped down on the sofa and turned the television on. Nothing happened. Joe sighed, got up and went into the kitchen. He decided to make his favourite drink. He was just stirring it when there was a knock at the door. Joe opened it and couldn't believe his eyes.

(Answers to likely questions: Mum's car had broken down. There was a power cut. His favourite drink was banana milkshake. A well known television presenter was at the door because Joe's mum had won a prize.)

2 Gemma followed the others outside. She went and stood by the wall, and munched her apple. It was quite warm in the sunshine. One group was playing tag on the grass. Others were skipping, or kicking a ball around. No one else seemed to be on their own. Suddenly, something whizzed over her head and landed on the other side of the wall. A few seconds later Gemma heard the sound of sobbing. 'Why did he do that, it's my best one', cried the voice. 'My mum will be mad if I don't take it home.' The voice was coming nearer. Two of the others had their arm round her. Gemma beckoned to them.

(Answers to likely questions: She is at a new school. It is playtime and she doesn't know anyone. One of the children has thrown a soft toy over the wall. Gemma knows where it landed and wants to tell them. It will be a good way to make friends.)

3 Nita and Zep were staying with their Nan in the country. One afternoon, they climbed over the wall into the wood at the back of the house. They walked along the path for a while. Zep stopped. 'That's funny', he said. 'I didn't notice it last time we came this way.' Nita bent down and picked it up. 'I wonder where it goes,' she said. They walked on in silence until they reached the empty cottage. Nita looked at Zep. 'Shall we try it?' she said, nervously. At that moment they heard a sound in the undergrowth. Something was coming nearer, snapping twigs and branches as it did so. 'Quick, Nita', hissed Zep, 'It's our only hope.'

(Answers to likely questions: Zep spotted a key on the ground. They wondered if it was the key to the empty house. They are frightened and don't want to come face to face with the creature or person they can hear approaching. They decide the best thing is to open the door and hide in the house.)

Ask Me a Question *(continued)*

Stage IV

Active Listening & Memory

4 Jess was late for school. It wasn't her fault. The clock batteries were dead and anyway he always woke her, every single day. So why not today? She didn't bother to brush her teeth or hair. There was no time to make a sandwich. That meant she would need some money for the canteen. He would have to let her have some money for the school canteen for once. She grabbed her bag and ran downstairs. She paused outside his door, then knocked. No answer. She called out. No answer. So she opened the door and looked into his empty room. Slowly she picked up the folded piece of paper from the table. After she had read it she stood still for a second, then grabbed the phone.

(Answers to likely questions: 'He' is her older brother. Their parents are visiting relatives abroad. Her brother got caught stealing food from a supermarket, but managed to run away. He is hiding at a friend's house. Jess phones the friend.)

5 The boys were excited as they saw the coach pull up. Mr Stubbins ticked everyone off on a list as they got on. Soon the jostling queue of boys was seated in the coach, but Mr Stubbins was still standing with his clipboard, chewing the top of his pen and looking anxiously up and down the road. 'Sir, sir, we're going to be late', exclaimed the boys in the front seat. 'I can't go without them', replied Mr Stubbins. Suddenly a jingly tune started, and he looked around in alarm. The boys in the front seat giggled. 'It's yours, Sir! Look in your pocket.' Mr Stubbins fumbled in his jacket pocket, but he was too slow. The jingling had stopped. 'See who it's from', said the boys. 'How do I do that?' he answered.

(Answers to likely questions: They are going to watch a football match but two of the team haven't arrived. Mr Stubbins' mobile rings but he doesn't recognise the ringtone. He doesn't know how to dial a missed call.)

Stage IV

Active
Listening &
Memory

Ask Me a Question *(continued)*

6 Mrs Jolly worked fast as she sat in her chair by the window. She hoped she would get it finished in time for Saturday. There was still the whole of one side to do, and then the whole thing needed pressing. A slight noise in the corner near the bookcase made her look up. 'Oh no', she thought, 'I hope it hasn't got in again.' She kept looking nervously towards the little hole in the skirting board. At the same time she tucked her feet up so they weren't touching the floor. A few minutes later there was a knock on the window. Mrs Jolly could see her neighbour's 10-year-old daughter outside, mouthing something to her which she couldn't quite hear. 'Seen your what, dear?' said Mrs Jolly as she opened the window.

(Answers to likely questions: She is making a christening robe for her granddaughter. There has been a mouse in the room several times. It comes through the hole in the skirting board. Mrs Jolly hates mice. Her neighbour's daughter has lost her pet hamster and wonders if Mrs Jolly has seen it.)

Word Alert (3)

1 Jack woke up at *six thirty* on Saturday. He was excited because his dad
was taking him to a football match. *As soon as* he was dressed he raced
downstairs. '*When* are we leaving, Dad?' he asked. 'In about *half an
hour*', replied his dad. Jack switched the television on but he couldn't
concentrate. *After a while* he turned it off and stood by the door,
waiting. (5 points)

2 The Porter family was going on holiday. *At last* the day had arrived and
they set off for the airport. It took *ages* to check in the luggage and *then*
they sat around for at *least an hour* until their flight was called. *Finally*
they boarded the plane and *soon* it was soaring above the clouds. *In no
time* the cabin crew were telling them to prepare for landing and a *few
minutes later* they were on the tarmac, eight hundred miles from home.
(8 points)

3 *One summer day* Ricky and Joe decided to make a den. *First* they
collected some bits of wood that were lying around by dad's shed. *Then*
they found an old blanket that mum was going to take to the rag bank.
They took it all down to the end of the garden. *Before* they chose a good
place they stopped for a *few minutes'* rest. *Then* it was back to work.
They found a gap in the hedge and *soon* they had put up the frame.
Next they draped the blanket over the frame. Inside it was quite cool and
shady. Maybe *that night* they could sleep out there? (9 points)

4 Boiling an egg is easy. *First* you need to put a pan of water on to boil.
When it is boiling carefully put an egg into the water. It will need to boil
for about *four and a half minutes. While* you are waiting, get an egg cup
ready and make a piece of toast to go with it. *Then* turn off the cooker
and lift the egg out of the water. Eat it *straight away* with the toast and
don't forget to wash up *after* you have finished. (7 points)

Word Alert (3) *(continued)*

5 Scruffy the puppy was filthy. He had spent *the whole morning* chasing butterflies round the garden, which involved charging in and out of a lot of puddles. *Then* he had jumped on top of a pile of grass clippings, so his fur was covered in mud and bits of grass. *After* Maisie finished her lunch she called the puppy. *When* she saw how dirty he was she decided he needed a bath. *First* she ran some water into the bath, *then* spread an old towel on the floor. She was *just about* to put Scruffy in the bath when the phone rang. *By the time* she had finished talking to her nan, Scruffy was nowhere to be seen. (8 points)

6 *Last year* we went to Spain for our holidays. We had booked a three-star hotel but *when* we arrived there had been a flood at the hotel, so we were given rooms in a very posh five-star one. *On the first morning* we explored the town. *Then* we had lunch in a little restaurant overlooking the harbour. *After lunch* we walked down to the beach and lay in the sun *for a while*. *That evening* we had dinner at the hotel and spent *the evening* watching the sun go down. We didn't get to bed until *after midnight*. (9 points)

7 I live about *ten minutes'* walk away from my school. I leave the house at *8.30 each morning*. *When* I get to the end of our road, I meet my friend Rosco and we walk the rest of the way together. The bell goes at *8.50* and we have to line up *before* we can go into class. The first bit of the *morning always* seems long. Maybe it's because we do Maths. *Then* it's break time, thank goodness. *After* break we usually do Literacy, which lasts until *lunch time*. (11 points)

8 *Last Saturday* our school played in a netball match. It started at *two o'clock*. Our team scored five goals in the *first half*. Then it was *half time*. During the *second half,* the other team started to score and *for a while* it was a draw. Luckily we scored again in the *last few minutes* and managed to win. *By the time* we got home we were exhausted. (8 points)

Story Map

Stage IV

Active
Listening &
Memory

who?

where?

what happened?

Story Map *(continued)*

Practice Story – Mrs Nibble lived in a small cottage with her two cats, Bonzo and Bruno. The cats were both black and each had four white paws. It was a white cottage, with a pretty garden full of flowers at the front. One day Mrs Nibbles was busy weeding the garden. Bruno and Bonzo were lying asleep in the sun. Suddenly there was a funny noise in the apple tree. A huge green parrot was sitting in the tree, saying 'Where's my lunch?' over and over again.

1 Harry and Sam were staying with Uncle Joe. Uncle Joe lived in a flat at the top of a big house. You had to walk up four flights of stairs to get to it. Once you got up there it was really cool, with a huge television and two white leather sofas. There was a roof garden full of weird tropical plants and that was where Joe's pet lived. Pandora was a large blue and green parrot who could talk. That Wednesday afternoon Harry and Sam puffed their way up the stairs, looking forward to having a chat with Pandora. When Joe opened the door he looked very upset. 'It's Pandora', he said. 'She's gone!'

2 Mr Bloggs parked his car in the garage and took the shopping bags out of the boot. He walked up the path and opened the door of his bungalow. The first thing he did was feed the cat, then he unpacked the shopping. He was in a hurry because it was Miss Timms' birthday and she was coming round for tea. He was just about to switch on the oven, when the house was plunged into darkness.

3 Matt and Kali were on holiday. They were staying in a caravan with their parents. The caravan was in a field, not far from the beach. They could see the sea from the caravan and it only took five minutes to walk down the track that led to Sandy Bay. They packed a picnic, collected their fishing nets and buckets and set off. They put the picnic bag in a shady patch and tried to catch shrimps in the rock pools. What they didn't notice was the large seagull who swooped down, poked at the picnic bag and flew off with two doughnuts in his beak.

Story Map *(continued)*

4 Kyle lived with his dad, in a flat near the train station. Kyle's Auntie Ellie lived in the flat next door and she gave him a skateboard for his ninth birthday. Kyle loved his skateboard and he and his friends used to practise every night in the summer and at weekends. They met in a little car park. It was always empty after six o'clock because the people in the offices had gone home. They had a brilliant time zooming round the tarmac, learning new stunts and showing off to each other. One warm summer evening Kyle turned up as usual, but a gate had been put up with a sign saying 'No Skateboards Here!'

5 It was a bright spring morning and Josh was in the park waiting for his friends, Tom and Zack. They all had scooters and it was really good fun zooming down the steep path that led from the little wood at the top of the park to the boating lake at the bottom. While he waited, Josh watched a grey squirrel running up and down the branches of an oak tree. The oak tree was at the very top of the park. From there Josh could see the sloping tarmac path, with the lake glinting in the distance. At last his friends arrived and they set off down the path, going faster and faster. Just as he reached the turn at the bottom, a football appeared from nowhere and Josh skidded to avoid it. The last thing he remembered was seeing the glinting surface of the lake coming closer and closer.

6 Katie was searching in the rough grass at the edge of the playing field. She had lost the back door key, so she couldn't get in to the house. The last time she had the key was when she was saying goodbye to Sam and Josie. They had been standing chatting for a while, half watching some boys playing football. Mum wouldn't be back from work until after four o'clock and it would be dark by then. Katie walked through the long grass, bent double, peering at the damp leaves. It was getting cold and had just started to rain. She began to feel panicky. She had left her mobile in the house, so she couldn't even phone mum. Then something caught her eye; something was glowing in amongst the leaves.

Stage IV

Active
Listening &
Memory

Story Map *(continued)*

7 Mrs Tripp was in her garden, weeding the vegetable patch. It was a hot day and she noticed how dry the soil was. The leaves of the lettuces and carrots had gone limp and there were patches of dead grass on the lawn. She decided to get out the hose and give the vegetables a good soaking. There was no outside tap, so she fixed the hosepipe to the tap in the kitchen. Then she walked up and down the rows of thirsty plants, spraying them with the hose. Mr Evans leant over the fence to say hello, and Mrs Tripp put the hose down so that the water would soak the lawn while she chatted. When they had finished talking she went inside to turn the tap off, only to discover that the hosepipe hadn't been fitted on the tap properly and water had been squirting out sideways all the time.

8 Jamilla was standing at the bus stop waiting for the school bus. It was a cold foggy morning and all the cars had their headlights on. There were four other people in the queue and everyone looked cold and fed up. They waited and waited, and then finally a bus appeared, but it wasn't the Number 24, and it had an 'L' plate on the front. The man sitting beside the young driver leant over and said, 'Sorry, he's just a learner – can't take passengers yet! Number 24's late because of all this fog.' The waiting passengers sighed as the bus drove off. Then, to Jamilla's delight, she recognised the blue car approaching. Her best friend had obviously persuaded her dad to drive her to school. Jamilla waved frantically and the car slowed down.

No!

Stage IV

Active Listening & Memory

1 The Sludgy Canal clearing project today reported a great success. A long mile stretch has been re-opened to shipping. This stretch includes several six-metre high bridges, a watermill, and a lock. The first yacht in 30 years to navigate this canal tied up at Maltings Mill on Tuesday afternoon. She is the yacht *Bluebell*, a Flower Class boat with a 10m mast. *(A 10m mast could not get under the bridges.)*

2 Ten marathon walkers set out at midday on Saturday, to try to beat the record of 48 hours from Tower Bridge to Land's End. The first man to arrive, Jim Quick from Portsmouth, arrived at the Tourist Centre at Land's End at half-past two on Monday, to be greeted by cheering crowds. He now holds the record.

3 Some of the children from Great Puddle Primary School have taken part in a painting competition. The competition was open to children aged from six to eight years, and the choice of subject included 'A Snow Scene', 'A Circus' and a 'Street Fair'. Tariq (aged nine) walked away with the first prize, for his exciting and brightly coloured street fair. He was thrilled with his computer game.

4 The local paper (the *Weekly Screech*) today published a list of all the local events that had been enjoyed by the community throughout the year. The Mayor, Mr Butterball, said it was a credit to all the organisers, and showed that community spirit was alive and well. Among the highlights recorded were the welly throwing contest in January, the Flower Show in December, and the Vintage Car rally in October.

5 The Topnotch Maternity Hospital today claimed the first baby to be born in the New Year. Bouncing baby Cheryl arrived at one minute past midnight. Proud parents Rick (29) and Candy (82) said they were overjoyed. 'This is the best start to the New Year we could possibly have', said Rick. 'We hope to take her home later today.'

Stage IV

Active
Listening &
Memory

No! *(continued)*

6 To the great regret of all the local people, their corner shop is to close
down at the end of the summer, 60 years after it was founded by Mr and
Mrs Patel. 'The shop has been a real blessing', said Mrs Jackson, of
nearby Ashton Villas. 'You can get almost anything there, and the Patels
are so helpful. They will even bring things round to the house if you are ill
and ring them up.' Mr Patel said he was taking early retirement, although
he is only 55. 'We have worked our socks off since we started the shop',
he said, 'And now we are looking forward to a rest.'

For and Against

1 The council is discussing whether or not to build a skateboard area on the recreation ground. If they decide to go ahead, it will mean an increase in the number of older children using the recreation ground. This could be off-putting to mothers and toddlers who want to use the swings and slides. Gangs of skateboarders are likely to be noisy and will probably leave litter lying around. Building a skateboard area will reduce the amount of grass on the playing field.

(Against)

2 The head teacher wants to start school half an hour earlier each day, at 08.30 instead of 09.00 although a lot of parents disagree. If school started at 08.30, the children could go home at 14.30. This means they would have much longer at home to play with their friends and be with their families. In the winter they would not have to walk home in the dark. In the summer there would be time to go out after school.

(For)

3 A member of parliament said children should choose their own bedtime. Adults often tell children they are tired, when actually it is the adults who are tired. Children know how they feel. They know when they need to go to bed. If they are sent to bed too early, they get cross and fed up. They might start fighting with their brothers and sisters. If they go to bed when they feel tired, they will go to sleep quickly and get a good night's sleep.

(For)

4 Lots of parents get worried about having a pet. They think the children will get bored with it. But children love pets. They can learn a lot about caring for animals and taking responsibility. They can also learn about how different kinds of animals live, and which countries they come from. Pets can teach children to be considerate and kind and can be very comforting if you are ill or sad.

(For)

Stage IV

Active
Listening &
Memory

For and Against *(continued)*

5 Parents worry about how much time their children spend playing computer games. Kids think computer games are really cool. You can't really communicate with a computer though. You can't talk to your friends, even if you are playing the same game. Sometimes it's good to talk to friends, especially if you are worried, or things at home are not good. You need to get used to talking to them though, and that takes practice. If you always play computer games with your friends, you won't get much practice at just talking about things.

(Against)

6 They are going to scrap school uniform at our school. No more boring green sweatshirts! Instead we can choose exactly what we want to wear. The trouble is my mum can't afford really cool trainers and tops. I kind of told my friends that I had loads of pairs of cool trainers at home and now they are going to find out that I've only got the cheapest ones. Then there's all the other cool stuff. Mum gets most of our clothes from charity shops, or her friends' older kids.

(Against)

7 There is going to be a new rule at our school. We can choose how long it will take us to do our homework. That means if it's a subject we like, we can really get into it, do all the research and spend time making it look good. That way we will get to know the subject even better. It's annoying to have to rush something just because it has to be handed in tomorrow.

(For)

8 Our school canteen is going to change over to a healthy eating policy. It will only serve organic foods and they will cost more money. This means some kids won't be able to have food from the canteen. Organic food is better for us and the more people that buy it, the cheaper it will get. It is better to have food that is better quality in smaller quantities. This may help the growing problem of obesity in children.

(For)

Training Sessions

1 Good balance. Likes working on his own. Good head for heights. Good with his hands. Strong. Agile. (Steeplejack)

2 Good balance. Strong. Likes a travelling life. Likes to have an audience. No fear of heights. (Trapeze artist)

3 Good at science. Likes helping people. Not scared by blood. Likes studying how the body works. (Surgeon)

4 Likes being out of doors. Interested in plants and flowers. Strong. Doesn't mind working on his own. (Gardener)

5 Likes travelling and seeing the world. Enjoys working as part of a team. Likes the sea and boats. (Sailor)

6 Loves speed. Understands how engines work. Fearless. Quick reactions. Likes to win. (Racing driver)

7 Adventurous. Interested in outer space. Doesn't mind living in a confined area. Easy to get on with. Very fit. Good with machinery. (Astronaut)

8 Adventurous. Doesn't mind living rough and facing danger. Fit. Interested in maps. Happy to be on his own. (Explorer)

Stage I

Thinking & Reasoning

Riddle-me-ree

What has a tail and can fly, but isn't a bird? (kite, aeroplane, dragonfly)

What has four legs, but cannot walk? (table, chair)

What has two hands, but cannot hold anything? (clock, watch)

What has a bark, but isn't a dog? (tree)

What runs, but has no feet? (water, river, tap)

What has a face, but cannot see? (clock, watch)

What sort of roll stays still? (jam roll, swiss roll, sausage roll)

What keeps on falling, but doesn't hurt itself? (waterfall)

What kind of mouse doesn't eat cheese? (computer mouse)

What gets up in the morning, but doesn't have to get dressed? (sun, animals, birds)

Rescue!

You see a man in a mask breaking a shop window, and putting the jewellery from the window display into a bag. His car is parked in the street just beside him.

(Would you: Tackle him? Run for help? Go and phone the police? Note down the car number? Go and phone the shop owner?)

There is a cat stuck up a tree in the park. A dog is barking at the bottom of the tree.

(Would you: Go and see if you can find someone to bring a ladder? See if you can find the dog's owner? Climb the tree and try to get the cat down? Call the fire brigade?)

A little boy has been sailing his boat on a pond, and it has now floated away out of reach.

(Would you: Wade in and try to get it? Get a stick and try to reach it that way? Ask where his parents are? Go round to the side of the pond where the boat seems to be heading?)

You have got home, only to find that your parents are out, and you have somehow lost your key.

(Would you: Break a window and get in that way? Borrow a ladder and get in through an upstairs window? See if a neighbour has a key? See if Mum or Dad have left a key in the usual hiding place? Go to a neighbour and ask if you can stay there until your parents get home? Use your mobile, or borrow a phone, to try to ring Mum or Dad?)

You are in the house on your own, and a man you don't know rings the doorbell. He says he has come to fix a leaking pipe.

(Would you: Ask to see his identification badge? Let him in immediately? Tell him to go away? Pretend you don't know he is there? Call the police? Phone Mum or Dad if you can, to ask if they know about him?)

Stage I

Thinking &
Reasoning

Raceboard

General Instructions

1 This board has been designed for use in a variety of different games in this book. You will probably therefore need to make several versions of it.

2 Enlarge the board if necessary and laminate to protect it.

3 If a player lands on a ☆, they take a card from the pile and do what it says.

4 If a player lands on a ☺, they go forward one space.

5 If a player lands on a ☹, they go back one space.

6 These are only suggestions – you can alter them to suit the game and add any suitable embellishments to make it look more fun.

Raceboard

Stage I

Thinking & Reasoning

Stage I

Thinking &
Reasoning

Thinking Pairs

Ball, jug, scarf, CD, paint brush, sugar, scissors, chair, drum, towel, orange, bag, spoon, toothbrush, banana

It's round.	You can't eat it.
It holds liquid.	It's got a handle.
It's long.	It's made of fabric.
It's shiny.	You can listen to it.
It's got bristles.	It's long.
It's white.	It's sweet.
It cuts.	It's not a knife.
It has a back and legs.	It's not alive.
It's round.	You can bang it.
It's made of fabric.	You can't wear it.
You can eat it.	It's round.
It's got a handle.	You can put things in it.
It's shiny.	It's made of metal.
You use it every day.	It's got bristles.
It's sweet.	You can eat it.

Information Chain

Stage I

Thinking & Reasoning

candle	It's white.	It feels smooth.	It's a cylinder.	It's useful in the dark.	It's made of wax.
cushion	It's square.	It's made of fabric.	It feels soft.	It goes on a chair.	It can be any colour.
book	It's a rectangle.	It feels hard.	It has a cover.	It has words in it.	It's made of paper.
paper clip	It's made of metal.	It's small.	The metal is curved.	It fixes paper together.	There are lots in school.
torch	It needs a battery.	It has a switch.	It's useful at night.	You carry it.	It has a bulb.
umbrella	It has a handle.	It can fold up.	You carry it.	It can give shelter.	It's useful in wet weather.
egg	It's hard.	It's an oval shape.	You can eat it.	You need to cook it.	If you drop it, it will break.
apple	It's round.	It's smooth.	It's edible.	It has pips.	It comes from a tree.
socks	They come in pairs.	They are made of fabric.	They can be any colour.	They feel soft.	You wear them on your feet.
towel	It's a rectangle.	It's made of fabric.	It's very absorbent.	You use it after washing.	It feels soft.
hoop	It's round.	It's light.	It's made of plastic.	It can be used in PE.	You can climb through it.
packet of crisps	It's very light.	It's a container.	It contains edible things.	It may be in your lunchbox.	The contents taste salty.

Understanding & Using Spoken Language © C Delamain & J Spring 2004

Stage II

Thinking & Reasoning

Explorers

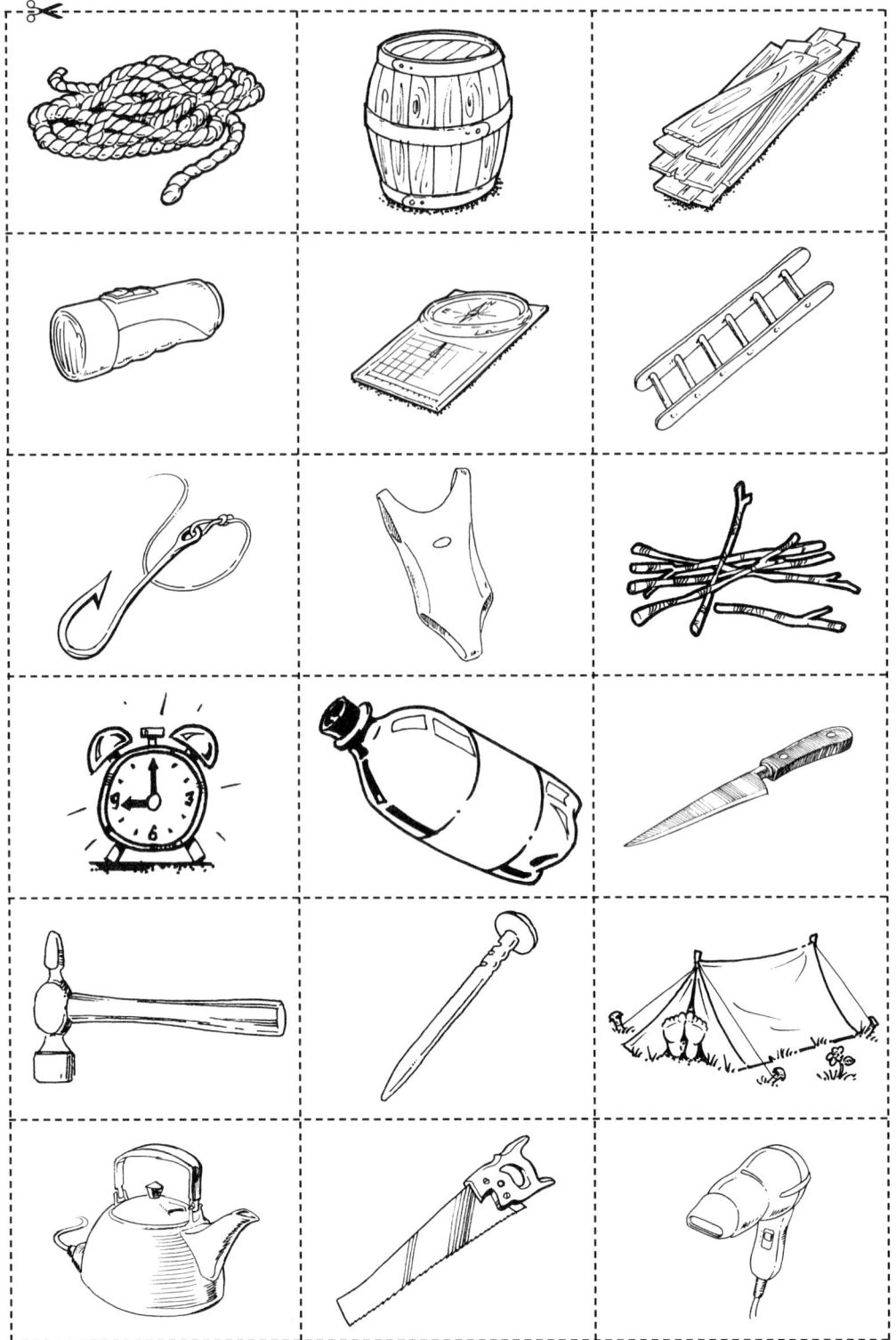

Mysterious Meanings

Stage II

Thinking & Reasoning

I'm in deep water here.
1 I'm out of my depth in the pool.
2 I'm drowning.
3 I'm in a complicated situation that I don't know how to cope with.

You're too big for your boots.
1 The hiking boots you are trying on don't fit.
2 You've outgrown your wellingtons.
3 You're too self-confident and pleased with yourself.

Pull your socks up.
1 Your socks are coming down.
2 You need to try harder.
3 Stretch your socks so they get longer.

A fish out of water.
1 Being in a place you are not comfortable in.
2 A fish that has run out of water to drink.
3 A fish that has been stranded on dry land.

He's away with the fairies today.
1 He's been kidnapped by fairies.
2 He's daydreaming and not concentrating.
3 He's acting in a pantomime.

She's feeling a bit under the weather.
1 She's feeling around for something in wet soil.
2 She's standing under a massive rain cloud.
3 She's not feeling very well.

He's got green fingers.
1 He's a good gardener. All his plants grow well.
2 He's got green paint on his hands.
3 He's probably a monster from outer space.

That house has changed hands dozens of times.
1 That house keeps growing new hands.
2 That house keeps taking off its hands and swapping them over.
3 That house has been bought and sold very often.

Stage II

Thinking &
Reasoning

Fact Finders

1 What is the capital of Italy?

2 Which part of a plant is below the ground?

3 Name four different bones in the human body.

4 What does *transparent* mean?

5 Who did England fight in World War Two?

6 Why do cars have rubber tyres?

7 Name three countries in Africa.

8 Which planet is furthest from the sun?

9 What does a plant need to grow?

10 Name four different materials.

11 Which warrior queen did the Romans fight?

12 What river flows through Egypt?

13 What happens to salt if you put it in water?

14 Which organ pumps blood around your body?

15 Name three things you could find in a rock pool?

16 Which planet is bigger; Mars or Venus?

17 Which country did the Vikings come from?

18 What is the name of the force that keeps our feet on the ground?

19 What does *ancient* mean?

20 What is the name of the ocean between the USA and Africa?

Think Hard!

1 What is half of 10?

2 Joe caught the first three fish, Sam caught the next eight. How many fish altogether?

3 Think of an even number between 75 and 90.

4 What is half of a half?

5 Which month comes after the fourth month of the year?

6 Lisa and Ben shared a six-pack of cola equally. How many cans each?

7 How many legs do four cows have altogether?

8 Which year came first, 1492 or 1942?

9 How many sides does an octagon have?

10 Think of an odd number between 60 and 90.

11 What do two quarters make?

12 Which is the seventh month of the year?

13 Double 30.

14 How many 10s are there in 150?

15 How long is a fortnight?

16 The train leaves at 2.30 and the journey takes one hour. What time will it arrive?

17 I bought two apples, seven pears and three oranges. How much fruit altogether?

18 Which year came first, 1971 or 1791?

19 What is half of 50?

20 Four friends are sharing a pizza. How much will they have each?

21 Which is heaviest, one kilo or 850 grams?

22 How many pence are in £1.35?

Stage III

Thinking & Reasoning

Phone Call

1 'Have you had your stitches out yet?' (The plumber, the vet, **someone who has had an operation**, the dressmaker.)

2 'I need to look good for the party on Friday.' (Supermarket, **hairdresser**, Granny, doctor.)

3 'It's pouring out from under the sink.' (Vicar, doctor, grand-daughter, **plumber**.)

4 'You sent the wrong catalogue number and the wrong size.' (Dentist, carpenter, **mail order company**, police station.)

5 'The window's open and there's a pane broken.'(**Police station**, carpenter, builder, electrician.)

6 'He's been off his food for three days, and doesn't even want to go for a walk.' (Doctor, **vet**, dentist, teacher.)

7 '…and three slates blew off in the gale.' (Granny, **builder**, caretaker, library.)

8 '…miles from anywhere, and my left front tyre is completely flat.' (Garage, **AA or RAC**, police, tyre shop.)

9 'It was a great party, wasn't it, so many old acquaintances, and wonderful food.' (Supermarket, **friend**, coffee shop, house agent.)

10 '…expecting this package for days, and there's no sign of it.' (Auntie, supermarket, library, **post office**.)

Speechmark

Ferryboat

Stage III

Thinking & Reasoning

To start with, use the example given on the Activity Sheet explaining, carefully who might eat what, and therefore who must not be left alone. Play the game once. After this first example, and when the principle is understood, just tell the children who they are (stick on labels if necessary as before) and let the ferryman work out the solution for himself.

Examples

- A fox, a chicken, a sack of corn, an oil drum and a joint of meat.

- A boy, a bag of chocolate bars, a big box of cough medicine, a canary and some birdseed.

- A monkey, a bunch of bananas, a lollipop, a cat and a boy.

- A basket, some honey, Winnie the Pooh, a crocodile and a cup of tea.

- A tortoise, some cabbage, a cat, some lettuce and a rabbit.

- A man, a sandwich, a mug of beer, a worm, a can of sardines and a bird.

- A bucket of fish, a sea-lion, a bundle of hay, a horse and a girl.

Stage III

Thinking &
Reasoning

Hidden Messages

Code Key

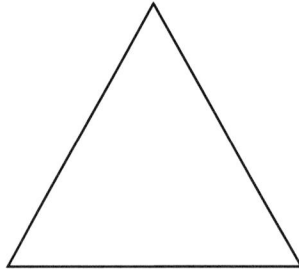

count

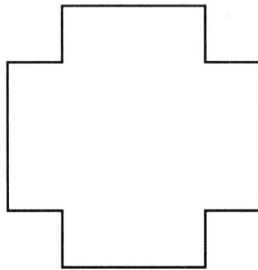

touch

look at

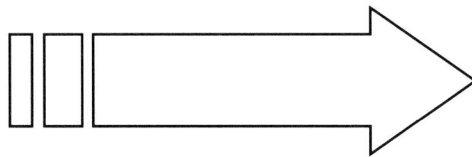

walk to

Speechmark Ⓟ

Hidden Messages *(continued)*

Stage III

Thinking & Reasoning

Walk to the door.	**Walk to the window.**	**Walk to the desk.**
Touch the door.	**Touch the window.**	**Touch the desk.**
Look at the floor.	**Look at the door.**	**Look at the window.**
Touch your nose.	**Touch your hair.**	**Touch your knee.**
Count to 5.	**Count to 11.**	**Count to 20.**

Stage III

Thinking &
Reasoning

Hidden Messages *(continued)*

the door.	the window.	the desk.
the door.	the window.	the desk.
the floor.	the door.	the window.
your nose.	your hair.	your knee.
to 5.	to 11.	to 20.

Speechmark   **P** This page may be photocopied for instructional use only.

Alibis

Stage IV

Thinking & Reasoning

Bert is alleged to have painted a picture of a green Mickey Mouse® on the school fence.

Bert says: 'I didn't do it. I went straight home after school, on the school bus. My mum was at home, and she can tell you I stayed in the rest of the day doing homework and watching telly.'

Facts:
- The mouse picture was not there at dinner time.
- It was seen at four in the afternoon.
- Bert took part in a rehearsal between dinner time and home time.
- Bert lives six miles from school, and it takes three quarters of an hour to get home.

(Bert is innocent.)

Joe Bloggs is said to have taken a sugar bun from the counter in the bakery at two minutes to three.

Joe says: 'I had a look round, and I bought a chocolate cake for £1.50. I went out of that shop at five past three. I saw the time on that big clock in the square. I just got a Poole Park bus as it was leaving.

Facts:
- The chocolate cakes in the shop do cost £1.50.
- Poole Park buses leave on the hour and half hour.
- The clock in the square has been broken for a month.

(Joe Bloggs is guilty and traces of sugar were found in his pocket!)

Bill the Burglar is said to have stolen a bird table from outside his local pet shop, at some time on the afternoon of Thursday 12th April.

Bill says: 'I couldn't have done it. That Thursday I was doing odd jobs for Mr Black round the factory. I got in around half past one. I shifted the barrels like Mr Black had told me, and swept up the floors. On the way home I bought a cuppa from the hot drink stand outside the factory. I didn't get home until after shop closing time.

Facts:
- The factory opens at 1.30 for the afternoon shift.
- The barrels were moved out of the factory on 12th April.
- The hot drink seller knocked off at four o'clock as it was so cold.
- The pet shop closes at 6.30 in Spring and Summer.

(Bill the Burglar is guilty. The bird table was found propped up against his back door.)

Alibis *(continued)*

Honest John is said to have pinched the fishing rod from a garden gnome at Number 15.

The householder claims he saw a man resembling Honest John walking out of the garden, with the fishing rod sticking out of his pocket. The gnome's owner gave chase, but the man got away and was seen scrambling over a wall.

Facts:
- The thief was wearing jeans and trainers.
- Footprints in the garden were measured as size 10.
- Honest John takes size 10 shoes.
- Friends and colleagues of Honest John say they have never seen him wearing jeans or trainers.
- Honest John has a bad leg which causes him to limp.

(Honest John is innocent.)

Police suspect Dan of taking three lanterns from around roadworks in the street next to his home. They disappeared between midnight when the local policemen saw them, and the next morning.

Dan says he was in the Cat and Fiddle pub till 11.30 last night. The pub is miles away from the roadworks. He says he walked home without passing the roadworks, and got back to his digs well before midnight. He says his old bat of a landlady must have heard him come in.

Facts:
- The Cat and Fiddle is closed for re-decorating.
- Dan's landlady took her hearing aid out and went to bed early last night.
- Dan is a very fast walker.

(Dan is guilty.)

Len is charged with putting a baby's potty on top of the flagpole on the island in the boating lake.

Len denies it. He says: 'That potty turned up on the flagpole about 8 o'clock, after the boat company closed for the night, and I can't swim. So how would I get across? Anywhere, where would I get a potty from?

Facts:
- The boat hire company closes at 7.45.
- Len's mum had a baby about six months ago.
- There is a lifesaving certificate on Len's bedroom wall.

(Len is guilty.)

Junk Designer

Design Cards

Stage IV

Thinking &
Reasoning

a chair	a robot
a treehouse	a swing
a poster	a pencil-case
a box	a curtain
a badge	a hamster cage
a birthday card	a necklace
a kite	a purse
a baby's rattle	a Christmas decoration
a drum	a mobile
a bird table	a picture frame
a cat's toy	a small pond

Stage IV

Thinking & Reasoning

Junk Designer *(continued)*

Junk Cards

string	a piece of fabric
egg boxes	macaroni
a plastic bucket	some dried peas
shoe box	six pieces of thin wire
shiny paper	a lump of plasticine
plastic film containers	coloured tissue-paper
thin pieces of wood	large sheet of paper
thick pieces of wood	a roll of wallpaper
stones	a large cardboard box
a ball of wool	an empty paint tin
pieces of card	a plank of wood
a plastic bin liner	a long rope
a reel of cotton	

Who Wants to Know?

Questions and Answers

✂- -

A: Platform 10, over the footbridge.

Q: Can you tell me where the train for London goes from?

A: I'm sorry, we only have groceries and newspapers.

Q: Do you sell trainers?

A: No, I should take it to the police station if I were you.

Q: Did you see who dropped this purse?

A: I'm sorry, I've only got a £5 note.

Q: Excuse me, have you got any change for the parking meter?

A: Up to the end of the road, turn right, and it's on your left.

Q: Can you tell me how to get to the park?

A: No, he moved away about a year ago.

Q: Does Mr Snodgrass still live in this house?

A: I'm afraid you've just missed the last one.

Q: Can you tell me what time the next bus goes?

A: No, its OK, he belongs to that house over there.

Q: This dog looks as if he's lost. Do you know where he comes from?

A: I'm sorry, I'm not a great reader, I've never been in there.

Q: Can you tell me if that bookshop is any good?

A: You can use my mobile if you like.

Q: Can you tell me where the nearest phone box is?

(These are roughly graded in order of difficulty.)

Stage IV

Thinking &
Reasoning

Take Away

MENU 1

Small dishes as starters
Grapefruit   Tomato soup
Small ham rolls with lettuce   Prawns with hot toast
Sardines

Main course
Crab salad   Roast beef and Yorkshire pudding
Sausages and mash   Chicken curry

Pudding
Treacle tart   Ice-cream and toffee sauce
Fruit salad   Apple pie

People
Mr Jones is allergic to shellfish. Mr Brown can't eat any pork products.
Miss Green and Mr Black can eat anything.

MENU 2

Small dishes as starters
Cheese on toast   Melon slice
Carrot soup

Main course
Vegetable curry   Baked potatoes with baked-bean filling
Chicken tikka masala   Sausage and chips

Pudding
Creamy chocolate pudding   Fruit salad
Fresh fruit   Stewed apple and custard

People
Mr Bates eats anything. Mrs Bates is trying to cut down on dairy
products. Miss Bates eats anything.

Speechmark

Take Away *(continued)*

✂- -

MENU 3

No starters

Main course

Steak and kidney pie	Egg and chips
Steak and salad	Egg curry
Beefburger and chips	Grilled chicken, beans and tomatoes

Puddings

Water ice	Apple fool
Sticky toffee pudding	

People

Mr and Mrs Diner eat anything. Miss Diner is trying to lose a bit of weight, so she is trying to avoid starchy foods and fat.

MENU 4

Soup starters

Vegetable soup	Fish soup
Chicken soup with cream	

Main courses

Prawn chop suey	Beefburger and chips
Lamb chops	
Steak and chips	Egg and bacon tart

Puddings

Lemon meringue pie	Creamy rice pudding
Jam pancakes	Chocolate sponge and custard

People

Mrs Picky doesn't like any meat except beef. Mr Picky dislikes any sort of fish. Miss Picky eats anything.

It will be easier for teachers to invent menus in the light of their knowledge of the children in their class. Encourage discussion about what the various dishes are, how nice they might be, and what the children themselves prefer to eat.

Stage IV

Thinking &
Reasoning

Sorted!

✂--

1 Miss Showbiz wants to produce an amateur play this summer. There
are only five people available who can really act. The best actress is
away in May, and the best actor in September. Of three possible plays,
one needs six good players and one needs only four. Miss Showbiz
doesn't want to upset anyone. The local hall has already been booked
through July and August. The stage is quite small and can't
accommodate a cast bigger than fourteen.

2 Mr and Mrs Globetrotter have arrived at the airport. They are just
getting near the head of the long queue to check in their baggage.
Mrs Globetrotter suddenly remembers that she has left her handbag in
the Ladies' Room. Mr Globetrotter very much wants to go to the
camera shop. Both of them need a cup of coffee. There are three
quarters of an hour before their plane is due to take off.

3 Tim Trainspotter is waiting behind two other people at the bus stop
with his suitcase. He is off to catch a train, and he thinks he will only
just make it if the bus to the station is on time. It is starting to snow,
and he has left his coat behind in the rush. There is a warm jumper in
his luggage, but he dare not start unpacking on the pavement, in case
the bus comes. There is a sort of bus shelter, but if he goes in to keep
out of the wind and snow, he might not see the bus coming.

4 Shirley Shubunkin has come into the living room to find her cat, Pickles,
with his paw resting on the edge of the fish tank, which is tipping
dangerously. Pickles has a fish in his mouth, there is one fish dead on
the floor, and another flapping and gasping and looking as if he might
die any minute. Butch, the dog, is coming along the hall, barking.

5 Bessie Babysitter is outside the Town Hall. She has little William in the
pram, and the dog on a lead. She needs to go into the Town Hall to
sort out her parking fine, but there are quite a lot of steep steps up to
the door, and there is no way she can get the big pram up there. She
can't leave the baby, and there's a big notice saying 'Dogs not allowed'.
The baby is yelling for his feed. Luckily, Bessie Babysitter has brought a
bottle with her. The Town Hall closes for lunch in 40 minutes.

Speechmark Ⓟ

Be Polite!

Stage IV

Thinking &
Reasoning

✂---

| Question: | What did you think of the fish pie? |
| Response: | It had a most unusual flavour. |

✂---

| Question: | Do you like my new hat? |
| Response: | It's wonderful. That blue really suits you. |

✂---

| Question: | How was the bread board we gave you for your wedding present? |
| Response: | It will be great to be able to use a different one for each day of the week. |

✂---

| Question: | Did you like the dress I wore for my fiftieth birthday? |
| Response: | It was very pretty: my granddaughter has one just like it. |

✂---

| Question: | I do hope we didn't stay too long. |
| Response: | Not at all: Ron had a nice little snooze in his chair while you were talking. |

✂---

| Question: | Do you like this homemade ice-cream? |
| Response: | Its simply yummy, can I have the recipe? |

✂---

| Question: | What about another holiday together this year? |
| Response: | I think we feel we'd like something a bit more restful, and we know you like to keep on the go. |

✂---

| Question: | Did you mind my borrowing your trainers? |
| Response: | No: I expect I'll get the tar marks out of them eventually. |

Stage I

Word Play

Plus or Minus Pairs

add	+
take away	–
plus	addition
minus	subtraction

Speechmark Ⓟ This page may be photocopied for instructional use only.
Understanding & Using Spoken Language © C Delamain & J Spring 2004

What a Muddle!

Incomplete sentences

Stage I

Word Play

I saw a…	(saw)
I see the…	(sea)
I lent my bat to a…	(bat)
We might meet some…	(meat)
This is a tale about the donkey's …	(tail)
Duck down behind your chair like a…	(duck)
The soldiers fought in the…	(fort)
There's some hair on that…	(hare)
He knows which is his…	(nose)
The tiger can pour from the jug with his…	(paw)
The pony's reins get wet when it…	(rains)

Stage I

Word Play

What a Muddle! *(continued)*

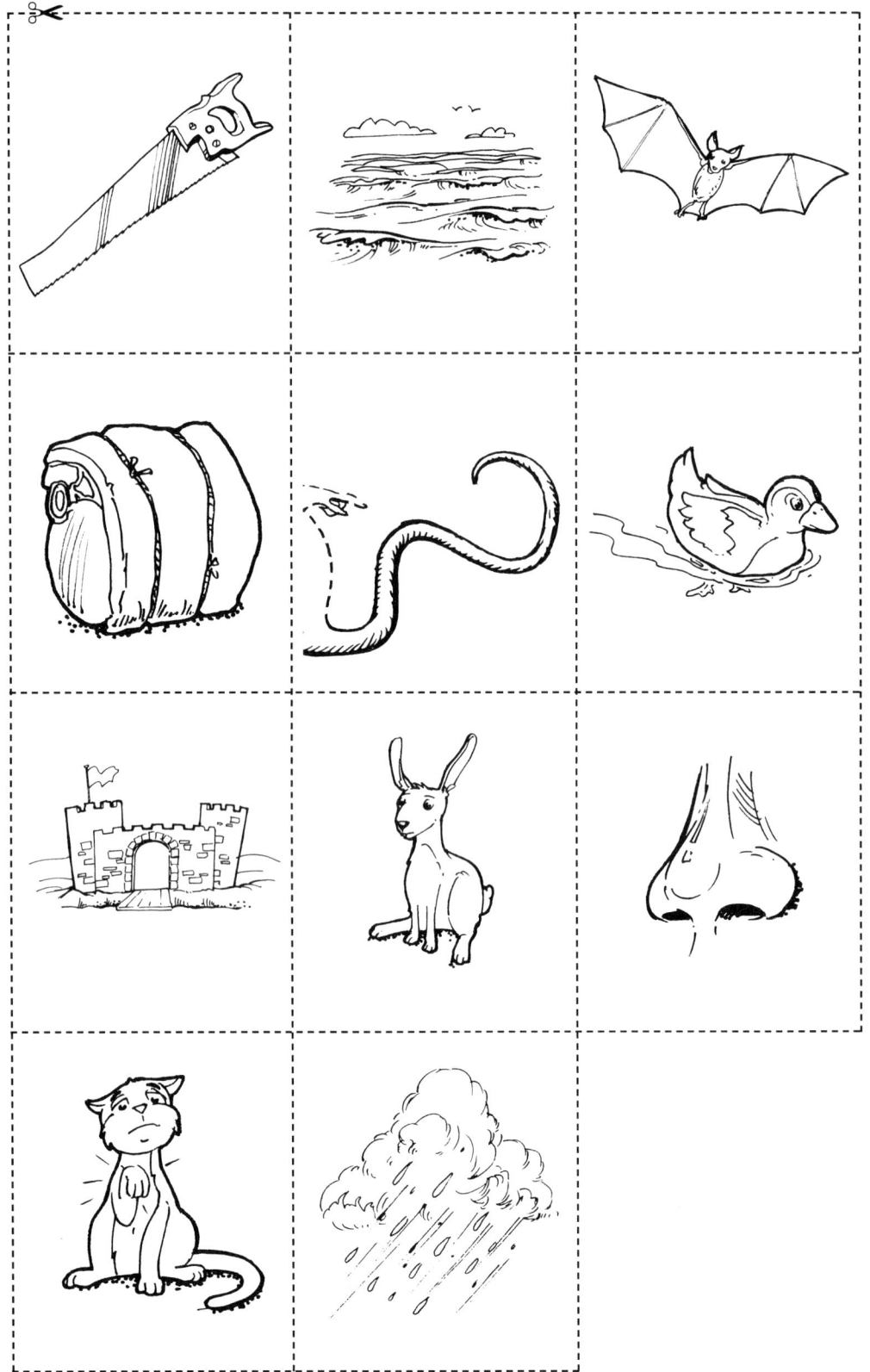

Speechmark Ⓟ This page may be photocopied for instructional use only.
Understanding & Using Spoken Language © C Delamain & J Spring 2004

Count the Sounds

Two-phoneme words

Three-phoneme words

Stage II

Word Play

Roots and Shoots

jump	paint
turn	light
pack	sense
cross	dress
group	foot
state	head
self	door
fish	cycle
time	stream
surf	screen

Gridlock (1)

Stage II

Word Play

✂--

Starter word: **Big**

Huge, Vast, Brilliant, Enormous, Colossal, Wonderful, Large, Tremendous, Great, Strong, Alarming, Monstrous, Wild, Elephantine, Immense.

Starter word: **Small**

Little, Tiny, Funny, Weeny, Miniscule, Sweet, Microscopic, Midget, Pocket-sized, Surprising, Weird, Diminutive, Miniature, Minute.

Starter word: **Pretty**

Beautiful, Lovely, Ravishing, Startling, Gorgeous, Good-looking, Attractive, Kind, Enchanting, Exquisite, Gentle, Smashing, Dishy.

Starter word: **Ugly**

Hideous, Unfriendly, Repulsive, Gruesome, Plain, Smelly, Disgusting, Revolting, Repellent, Unattractive, Foul-looking, Unsightly.

Starter word: **Frightening**

Scary, Terrifying, Loud, Weird, Spooky, Bad, Alarming, Spine-chilling, Unnerving, Ghastly, Unusual, Petrifying, Loopy, Horrifying.

Stage II

Word Play

Gridlock (1) *(continued)*

Speechmark ⑨ Ⓟ This page may be photocopied for instructional use only.
Understanding & Using Spoken Language © C Delamain & J Spring 2004

Vowel Detector (1)

| 'a' | 'e' | 'i' | 'o' | 'u' |

Stage II

Word Play

Stage II

Word Play

Vowel Detector (1) *(continued)*

'a'	'e'	'i'	'o'	'u'

Gridlock (2)

Stage III

Word Play

Starter word: **Gentle**

Rough	Cruel	Unkind	Horrid
Harsh	Fierce	Strange	Tough
Cunning	Severe	Dangerous	Hard
Brutal	Unpleasant	Violent	Squeaky

Starter word: **Quiet**

Noisy	Musical	Loud	Deafening
Booming	Tuneful	Banging	Hushed
Blaring	Roaring	Ear-splitting	Breaking
Thunderous	Crashing	Clanging	Echoing

Starter word: **Clever**

Stupid	Thick	Dumb	Mighty
Dim	Idiotic	Crafty	Halfwitted
Gormless	Mean	Dull	Mindless
Dense	Lazy	Daft	Bird-brained

Starter word: **Boring**

Exciting	Wonderful	Vivid	Useful
Gripping	Interesting	Silly	Stimulating
Inspiring	Rousing	Easy	Challenging
Startling	Difficult	Riveting	Exhilarating

Stage III

Word Play

Vowel Detector (2)

'ee'	'oo'	'ah'	'or'	'er'

Speechmark **P** This page may be photocopied for instructional use only.
Understanding & Using Spoken Language © C Delamain & J Spring 2004

Vowel Detector (2) *(continued)*

Stage III

Word Play

'ee'	'oo'	'ah'	'or'	'er'

1st

Understanding & Using Spoken Language © C Delamain & J Spring 2004

Stage III

Word Play

This Way and That

Verbs

run	walk	cry	laugh	scream
talk	eat	drink	fight	look
wash	move	dress	write	read
sing	march	choose	drive	play

Adverbs

quickly	silently	nastily	greedily	rapidly
slowly	swiftly	unkindly	hurriedly	quietly
steadily	loudly	reluctantly	heartily	hysterically
bitterly	softly	thirstily	frantically	endlessly
noisily	bravely	savagely	hastily	carefully
thoroughly	carelessly	sweetly	musically	happily
recklessly	dangerously	thoughtfully	firmly	smartly
neatly	prettily	speedily	sadly	heartbrokenly
helplessly	slurpily	messily	angrily	deeply
stiffly	sketchily	tunefully	raucously	peacefully
cheerfully	imaginatively			

Stage III

Word Play

Call My Bluff

Borborygmus (tummy rumbling due to gas in intestines)

Pobble

Outgrabe

Palaver (long drawn out discussion)

Skiggle

Quagga (recently extinct animal of the horse family)

Squoggy

Squiggle (a scribbled wiggly mark)

Voodoo (witchcraft, black magic)

Koodoo (kind of antelope)

Mangelwurzel (old-fashioned name for mangel or mangold, a kind of beet used for feeding cattle)

Mimble

Nubbly (covered with little lumps or bumps)

Brillig

Ogle (stare or gawp)

Ooshy-skooshy

Puffle

Piffle (nonsensical talk)

Slithy

Snickersnee (a large knife, especially one to use as a weapon

Snaggle-tooth (a sticking out or uneven tooth)

Scroodle

Stage IV

Word Play

Vowel Detector (3)

'ou'	'oa'	'oi'	'ay'	'eye'

Vowel Detector (3) *(continued)*

'ou'	'oa'	'oi'	'ay'	'eye'

Stage IV

Word Play

My Granny Said

A stitch in time saves nine.

Take care of the pennies and the pounds will take care of themselves.

The early bird catches the worm.

A bird in the hand is worth two in the bush.

All that glitters is not gold.

Many hands make light work.

Too many cooks spoil the broth.

No smoke without fire.

Out of sight, out of mind.

Absence makes the heart grow fonder.

One swallow doesn't make a summer.

Red sky at night, shepherds' delight:
red sky in the morning, sailors' warning.

Take it with a pinch of salt.

Fine words butter no parsnips.

Fix It!

mis-	take	fortune	lead
place	fit	trust	count
understand	behave	direct	un-
fortunate	happy	likely	kind
believable	friendly	comfortable	familiar
real	-ful	bliss	hope
care	thought	pain	help
tear	peace	use	tear
peace	use	fear	trust
-less	harm	use	care
hope	fear	end	thought
clue	pain	help	

Understanding & Using Spoken Language © C Delamain & J Spring 2004

Stage IV

Word Play

Gridlock (3)

The mouse crept into his _____ ,	but he couldn't get his _____ body in.
The children ate _____ sandwiches	while the car was stuck in the traffic _____ .
Tie this bit of string on to your big _____ ,	and see if you can _____ something along!
The photographer gave a _____ of despair	as the blue _____ spouted and dived under the waves.
Switch on the _____ and see	if that box is heavy or _____
The horse gave a buck and a _____	and his rider slipped off and landed on his _____

jam	hole	tow	whale
toe	light	wail	rear
jam	whole	light	rear

Speechmark (P) This page may be photocopied for instructional use only.
Understanding & Using Spoken Language © C Delamain & J Spring 2004

Gridlock (3) *(continued)*

Stage IV

Word Play

The _____ fought bravely, but	as _____ fell, it grew too dark to see.
The brown _____ shuffled through the leaves	under the _____ trees.
The _____ and drake had to ,	_____ to get under the low bridge.
It's _____ of you to buy these sweets	for me, but they aren't the _____ I like.
The _____ on the bus costs as much for a child as for an adult	and I don't think that's _____ .
Please will you _____ out these bricks by colour and size,	putting one _____ into each box.

bare	knight	kind	duck
sort	duck	fair	bear
night	fare	kind	sort

Gridlock (3) *(continued)*

The fisherman had to _____ into the stream	to get his fish, before it could be _____ in the competition.
Reach up with this _____ and see	if you can _____ that bit of wallpaper back on.
The _____ fall from the trees	as summer _____ and autumn arrives.
Try with all your _____,	and you _____ win the race.
_____ your letter, and make sure	you put the _____ address on the envelope.
Find a nice quiet camp _____,	within _____ of the sea.

wade	write	leaves	might
right	stick	sight	stick
might	leaves	site	weighed

Author!

1 The tiger seemed to be asleep. The keeper (walked) … as quietly as he could towards the sleeping animal (strolled, ambled, crept, pottered, tiptoed, sauntered, strode, marched, shuffled, sidled). As he approached, the tiger suddenly (got up) … (jumped up, leapt up, reared up, stood up, rose). With his heart in his mouth, the keeper (ran) … to the barrier (dashed, bolted, flew, fled, darted). The tiger lay down again and closed his eyes.

2 The two bullies were teasing poor Dave and pulling his hair. When Dave pleaded with them to stop, they just (laughed) … (sniggered, giggled, chortled, gloated, smirked, chuckled). They were so busy they didn't notice their maths teacher coming round the corner. 'Stop that this minute!' he (said) … (shouted, yelled, roared, muttered, howled, screamed, thundered). He (caught) … the ringleader with a swift movement (grabbed, snatched, seized).

3 As the knight rode up, the door of the castle slammed shut. The knight (knocked) … on the door with his mailed fist. (banged, hammered, beat, pounded, rapped, tapped). Nobody answered. The knight took hold of the huge handle and (pulled) … (tugged, yanked, heaved, hauled, strained). Slowly the door (opened) … (swung open, creaked open, inched open, groaned open).

4 Mathilda was making a fuss. She always did make a fuss about eating her greens. This time Mum was insisting. Mathilda (cried) … (sobbed, howled, wept, snivelled, sniffed, moaned), but it was no good. Then she began to (throw) … bits of broccoli about (fling, chunk, lob, hurl), until mum lost paience with her. Mathilda stared as Mum (put) … (tipped, scraped, shovelled, scooped) all the rest of her dinner into the bin. 'You can go without', she said.

5 Bonzo was enjoying his dinner. There was the usual plate of biscuit and meat, plus a juicy bone. Bonzo (ate) … (guzzled, gobbled, gnawed, chewed, chomped, nibbled) till the last bits were gone and his dish licked clean. Then he (lay down) … on his beanbag and went to sleep (nestled down, cuddled up, curled up, snuggled down). He seemed to be dreaming of chasing rabbits, as his whole body (moved) … (twitched, wriggled, shivered, shook).

6 Mr Crotchet was an unpleasant man. He liked things to go his way. He reached the bus stop just as the bus (drove off) … (pulled away, accelerated away, zoomed away, roared away). Mr Crotchet (complained) … (swore, cursed, raged, stormed, fumed). Seizing his bus ticket, he (tore it up) … (ripped it up, shredded it, screwed it up, destroyed it, decimated it) and threw it down on the pavement. Then, with a final curse, he walked off, while the other people at the bus stop giggled nervously.

Stage I

Explaining
& Describing

Adjective Ladder

Easy adjectives

big	sad
little	naughty
red	funny
blue	pretty
old	horrid
happy	kind
shiny	clever

Adjective Ladder *(continued)*

More difficult adjectives

Stage I

Explaining & Describing

enormous	aggressive
peculiar	expensive
amusing	talkative
intelligent	timid
generous	foolish
selfish	courageous
unpleasant	proud
elderly	genuine

Understanding & Using Spoken Language © C Delamain & J Spring 2004

Stage I

Explaining & Describing

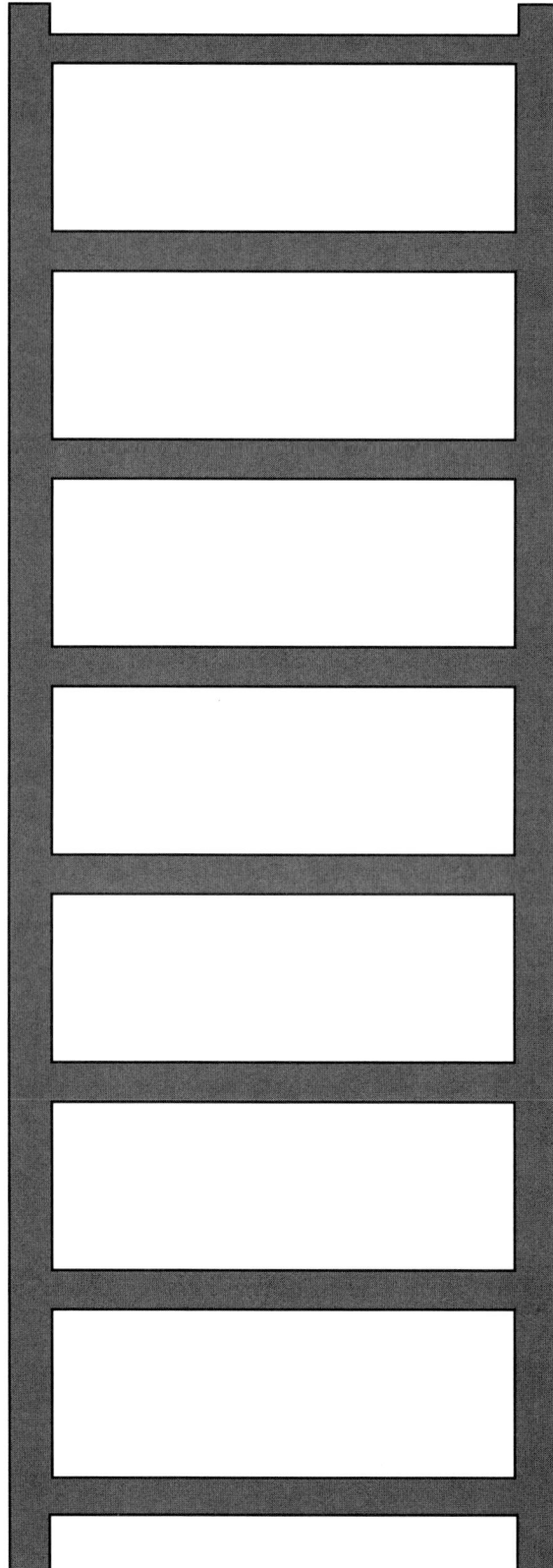

Adjective Ladder *(continued)*

Speechmark **P** This page may be photocopied for instructional use only.
Understanding & Using Spoken Language © C Delamain & J Spring 2004

Ifs and Buts

Mum does the shopping	I get scared
You can go outside	Teachers get cross
Children like playing	Snow is fun
Dogs bark	Boys play football
It's fun to have a picnic	I go to the shop
You will get very cold	Loud music is cool
It's OK to eat crisps	I feel happy
A cat purrs	Holidays are fun
Motorbikes go fast	Kittens are cute

Speechmark Ⓢ Ⓟ This page may be photocopied for instructional use only.

Understanding & Using Spoken Language © C Delamain & J Spring 2004

PAGE 245

Stage II

Explaining
& Describing

Ifs and Buts (continued)

if	but
so	**when**

Speechmark **P** This page may be photocopied for instructional use only.
Understanding & Using Spoken Language © C Delamain & J Spring 2004

Trailblazers

1 The travellers were making their way through a wood. They came to a place where the path divided into two, and the trailblazers had indicated that they should take the left-hand path. (*pause*) Before long, they found themselves walking at the base of a high cliff. The trailblazers had left a sign warning of falling rocks. (*pause*) Then the path began to wind upwards, and they came to a sign which indicated a beautiful view. (*pause*) They followed the sign, and found a spot which looked right out over the valley, across the river, to distant forests and hills. By late afternoon they had stopped climbing and reached the top: the travellers were exhausted. They were glad to find a sign indicating a picnic place, with drinking water available. (*pause*)

2 The man was driving his car in a foreign town. He turned left, having missed the sign showing it was a dead end. (*pause*) He backed the car with some difficulty, as there wasn't much room, and drove out into the main street again. He slowed down to 30 km per hour, as indicated by the sign, (*pause*) and pulled out. A sign showed that there were men digging up the road. (*pause*) There was the road he was looking for. He turned in, but was met by another problem – a large sign said 'No Parking'. (*pause*)

3 The family was off for a camping holiday on Dartmoor. It was an eventful drive. The first alarming sign showed that there might be animals crossing the road. (*pause*) The next indicated that the road often flooded, (*pause*) while the next showed a very, very steep hill. (*pause*) After about three hours, it was with relief that they saw the sign indicating the camp site ahead. (*pause*)

4 The mountain bus was on its way to the ski resort. The road twisted and turned continually, (*pause*) and then reached a long tunnel. (*pause*) As it emerged from the tunnel, a sign showed 'No overtaking', (*pause*) and as the road narrowed still further, another sign showed that traffic coming the opposite way took priority. The bus had to stop to let a line of cars come past. (*pause*)

Stage III

Explaining & Describing

Trailblazers *(continued)*

5 George was on a hiking holiday. He was making his way, via small lanes, across country towards the sea. He passed a sign indicating a nature reserve, and turned off his path to investigate. *(pause)* The reserve was full of interesting birds and butterflies. Towards lunchtime, he began to search for somewhere to get a drink and something to eat, and was glad to find a sign pointing to a café. *(pause)* After lunch his path wound downwards, and at the bottom a sign showed the way to some stepping stones, which led across a stream. *(pause)* As dusk began to fall, George realised he was not going to reach his destination before dark, and he began to look for somewhere to spend the night and get some breakfast the next morning. *(pause)*

Finish the Story

1 The plane was flying over snowy mountains when one of its engines failed. Then, to the pilot's horror, the second engine began to splutter. With great skill, the pilot found a clearing between the trees where the land was flat, and brought the plane down. Night was falling. The co-pilot, Bob, agreed to go to try to find help, while the pilot stayed to guard the plane. Bob set off through the snowy forest and, at long last, when he was nearly exhausted, he saw ahead of him:

- a little house with lights shining out
- a railway track
- a wellington boot
- another aeroplane with the key in the ignition
- a book of instructions for making lego models
- footprints in the snow

(Once the children have chosen what they think is the best of the options, encourage them to bring the story to a final conclusion – for example, if they choose the little house with the light shining out, ask them, 'So what happened then?')

2 Tom was watching television. At the end of the programme, there was an urgent news flash. A tiger had escaped from the local zoo, and was roaming somewhere in the countryside. It wasn't very sensible of him, but Tom fetched a torch, put on his boots, and went out into the dark night. He stood still and listened – nothing but the sound of cars from the nearby road, and once or twice an owl hooting. Then Tom froze. Something was moving in the bushes at the end of the garden. Pointing his torch, he saw:

- a hippopotamus
- the dog, trying to dig up an old bone
- the wind rustling the leaves
- Dad, planting onions
- two gleaming yellow eyes
- a man in zoo keeper's uniform, pointing towards the house.

Finish the Story *(continued)*

3 Ben was a bit bored one day after school. He was wandering around the streets near his house, when he noticed that one of the windows in a big warehouse was broken. The warehouse hadn't been used for ages, but now Ben could hear noises coming from inside. Quietly, he climbed in through the window, and hid behind a big stack of empty boxes. The noises were coming nearer and nearer. Suddenly round a corner appeared:

- a security guard
- three men in balaclavas, dragging a sack
- Harry Potter
- a massive dog
- Manchester United football team
- a teacher from his school.

4 Daisy and her friend had been paddling amongst the rocks at the seaside. The tide was coming in, but very slowly, and there were wonderful things to find in the rock pools. They were so busy fishing out shrimps and tiny crabs that they didn't notice that the tide had suddenly begun to come in faster. Small waves were beginning to break quite close to them. When Daisy next looked up, she gave a little shriek. Most of the rocks had disappeared, and there was now a stretch of deep water between them and the beach. 'Quick, quick,' Daisy said, 'We must take off our t-shirts and wave them, and shout. Someone will see or hear us.' At that moment they saw something on the surface of the water a long way away, but coming towards them. It was:

- a mermaid
- a battleship
- the lifeboat
- Uncle Jim, doing the crawl
- a giant octopus.

Speechmark Ⓟ This page may be photocopied for instructional use only.
Understanding & Using Spoken Language © C Delamain & J Spring 2004

Dangerous Mission

Stage II

Reporting
& Debating

The four tired men came to the edge of the forest, and found themselves at the top of a steep cliff. To their left, a path wound down in gentle curves. At its end was what seemed to be a marshy area, full of rushes. To the right, a much steeper path dropped down to the valley. ('Which path will the treasure seekers take?' Answer 1: The steep path.) The men slipped and slithered their way down the path, clutching at roots and boulders to save themselves from falling. When they reached the bottom of the valley, they found themselves beside a deep river, flowing swiftly, and full of swirling eddies and currents. A little way upstream, a fallen tree lay across the river. 'It was a bad day when we lost that rope', the leader said. 'Do we swim, or risk crossing that slippery tree?' (Answer 2: Cross by the tree.) One by one, they cautiously inched their way across the tree trunk. Just underneath them the water surged and gurgled. Jim missed his footing and nearly fell, but he righted himself, and joined the others on the far bank. Their relief turned to horror as they saw a huge lion facing them, less than 100 metres away. 'Quick decision, men,' said the leader. 'Back into the water, or stand our ground?' (Answer 3: Stand their ground.) The four stood steadily together in a tight group, their eyes meeting the eyes of the lion. After several minutes, during which they hardly dared breathe, the lion turned and slowly paced away.

'I know the map went the way of the rope', Bill said, 'But I remember we had to get up this side of the valley. The caves are up there. Should we add to the weight of our packs by filling our water-bottles from the river, or risk finding water at the top?' It looks quite green and lush up there,' Nick said. 'I vote we risk it. My pack feels as if I've got an elephant in it already.' (Answer 4: Risk finding water at the top.) The adventurers plodded their weary way up the hill.

The woods were full of strange noises – shrieks and squawks and rustlings – but by now the men were so tired they hardly noticed them. At the top the path branched, one way to the left, one to the right, and one straight on. 'These two look very overgrown, but that one looks as if it gets used quite often,' said Jack, pointing to the right-hand path. 'Should we take that one and risk being seen? At least we know it must go somewhere' (Answer 5: Take the right-hand path.)

Stage II

Reporting
& Debating

Dangerous Mission *(continued)*

Once the decision was made, they set off at a brisker pace. The way was flat and the walking easy between the trees, but as they rounded a bend, five or six savage-looking wild dogs rushed towards them. Like lightning, the four shinned up a tree each, dropping their packs at the bottom. The dogs prowled around the trunks of the trees, baying and snarling. 'Well climbed men!', called Jack, from the branches of his tree. 'Now I'll put it to a vote. Do we stay up here until these brutes give up and go away, or do we use our last anti-wolf kit? Lucky it's in my pocket. It should work just as well on these wild dogs, and we can't be far from the caves now.' (Answer 6: Use the anti-wolf kit.) The siren-like wailing of the anti-wolf kit sounded, and the dogs raced away, their tails between their legs.

The adventurers shinned down their trees and dusted themselves off. 'I seem to remember', said Jack, 'That the people hereabouts tend to stay indoors at night, with their houses shuttered and barred. So we'd be less likely to be spotted if we travelled by night for this last lap. On the other hand, it will be easier to find the cave by day. What do you reckon?' (Answer 7: Travel by night.) The idea of a bit of sleep, until night fell, was very welcome, and the men curled up under some bushes, well away from the path, and dozed until dusk.

It only took another half hour's walking to reach the cliff. As the map had shown, the cliff face was riddled with caves. 'Someone has had a fire in this one' Jim said. 'And it looks nice and dry.' 'But if people come there', argued Bill, 'We shan't be safe.'

'These others look very damp and drippy', said Nick. 'Well, make up your minds', Jack said. 'We're coming to the end of the adventure now'. (Answer 8: They chose one of the damp caves) 'Dare we light a fire?', wondered Jim. (Answer 9: Light a fire.) A good fire was soon blazing. 'Do you think we should brew up the last of the soup?' Bill asked, 'Or keep it for the return journey?' 'If we don't find the treasure', Jack answered, 'One tin of soup isn't going to save our skins'. (Answer 10: Use the soup.)

It was while he was exploring at the back of the cave that Jim bumped into something. He flashed his torch on to it. It was a rusty, dirty old chest. Jim drew a long breath. 'I believe we've found it', he whispered. 'What do we really think will be inside?' (Answer 11: Nothing!)

Newsreel (2)

Stage II

Reporting & Debating

✂--

1 Fire at sea. Crew all safe. Huge oil tanker ablaze. Captain missing. Crews took to lifeboats. Rescued by cruise liner. Ship sinking. Captain taken off by helicopter.

2 Family happy to have much-loved cat safely home. Fire brigade called. Fireman went up ladder with piece of fish. Cat found stuck up tree. Black and white cat lost.

3 Astronaut landed on Mars. Countdown heard all over the world. No messages received from spaceship for three days. Have met a real Martian! Scientists thrilled to get news on fourth day.

4 Aaron is only eight years old. Annual swimming contest held at local Olympic pool. The winner, Aaron North, has only been swimming for a year. Twenty-three competitors. Aaron's mother very proud.

5 21 January is Mrs Binn's birthday. Bingo played every Saturday in local hall. Mrs Binns has 14 grandchildren. Granny Binns 80 years old on 21 January. At Bingo Granny won £20.

6 Investigation showed branches of trees hitting windows. Ghost-hunters called to look into strange noises at Number 10 Elmtree Avenue. Family unhappy at strange noises heard in night. Every night odd tapping noises heard at window. Family pleased to be back at home with no worries.

7 Bike made from bits collected from second-hand ones. Taken two years to collect parts. Motor-bike race won by Billy Briggs. Billy's wife said he spent almost all his time in his workshop. Put parts together in the evening after work.

8 Two hundred letters received by zoo. Very hard to breed pandas in captivity. Sadly, baby panda died at two days old. Zoo keepers feeding baby with bottles. Ming-ming, giant panda, had baby on Thursday 2 April.

Stage II

Reporting & Debating

What Next?

1 Rory climbed over the fence into the field. It was cold and muddy and he kept slipping. He shone the torch in front of him. On the other side of the field he could see some sort of building…

2 Aleesha's mum gave her some money and told her to go to the shop and buy something for tea. While she was walking home, carrying the heavy shopping bag, the sky went very dark and large drops of rain started to fall…

3 Kerry and Lila always went to the park on Saturdays. They usually had a go on the swings and slides, and then bought an ice-cream. This week the ice-cream van wasn't in its usual place. Instead there was a van with 'Melissa Marvel's Magic Buns'…

4 Tilak lived with his mum and sister, Parvati, in a small flat. He shared a bedroom with Parvati. On morning he woke up and saw that Parvati's bed was empty. He went in to his mum's room. Mum was still asleep and Parvati was nowhere to be seen…

5 Connor loved football and he always watched his favourite team on television. One day he was in town and he saw a poster saying that his favourite team was playing at the local football ground on Saturday…

6 Gemma and Mark were staying at their Nan's house in the school holidays. The weather was awful – it rained every day. Nan told them to go up to the attic and find some of their mum's old games…

Text

Stage II

Reporting
& Debating

Messages:

1 'A man has fallen over the cliff near Swanage. We think he has broken
his leg. He is conscious, but in pain. Can you please scramble the
helicopter as soon as possible?' ('Man on cliff Swanage. Conscious,
broken leg, pain. Helicopter urgent.')

2 'I'm on the train, just coming in to Waterloo. The train is late, so I can't
meet you at 6 o'clock as we planned. I'll come straight to the flat,
arriving about 7 o'clock.'

3 'The ferry company has just said that all cross-channel boats have been
cancelled because of the stormy weather. I shall spend the night in a
hotel and try again tomorrow.'

4 Heavy traffic and road works on the M1 have caused long delays of up to
an hour. The AA and RAC suggest leaving the M1 at Junction 6 and
joining again at Junction 8, if possible.

5 The first cuckoo of the spring has been heard in a big wood near Brighton.
Several people have reported hearing the bird. This date, 25 March, is one
of the earliest dates on record for the cuckoo to come to Great Britain.

6 'May Samantha come and sleep-over with Jackie tonight please? Her Dad
and I have to go away, just for this one night. We didn't know about this
until just now. Please can you let me know if this is OK?'

7 'Mr Bumble's Circus is opening in London soon. There are loads of great
acts – my Dad saw it up North, two weeks ago. There are still some tickets
if you are quick: you can ring or text to book. Don't wait! Do it now!'

8 'Tim has got on the wrong bus by mistake! He will get to the bus station
earlier, at 5.30pm instead of 6 o'clock. You know what he's like; he will
get into a real panic if you aren't there to meet him, so please make sure
you are there. He hasn't got his mobile on him, so I can't let him know.'

If these messages are too hard to read, or too difficult to reduce to text
messages for the children concerned, re-phrase them or write new
messages. Feel free to change the place names to ones that the children are
familiar with.

Stage III

Reporting
& Debating

Celebrity

Drummin' Dave (Rock Star)

Food	Mayonnaise and chips
Hair	Ginger, spiky
Shops	Gadget Shop
Car	1970 Ford Fiesta
Sports	Football (Liverpool)

Mandy Malone (Singer)

Food	Crispy noodles
Hair	Shaved head
Shops	Monsoon
Car	Vintage Saab
Sports	Fencing

Fiona Fantasy (Supermodel)

Food	Lettuce leaves
Hair	Long, straight, black
Shops	Gucci, Spar
Car	Yellow Mini
Sports	Scuba Diving

Gemma Jump (Jockey)

Food	Sausage and mash
Hair	Short, black
Shops	Top Shop
Car	Land Rover
Sports	Horse Racing

Sir Peter Plonk (Company Director)

Food	Marmite on toast
Hair	White, curly
Shops	Harrods
Car	Rolls-Royce
Sports	Golf

Kev Stripe (Footballer)

Food	Bacon butties
Hair	Blonde dreadlocks
Shops	JJB Sports
Car	Audi
Sports	Snooker

Arty Artino (American film star)

Food	Steak and fries
Hair	Blonde, streaky
Shops	Tiffanys
Car	Jaguar
Sports	American football

Oscar Sable (Painter)

Food	Oysters
Hair	Long, ponytail
Shops	Oxfam
Car	MG
Sports	Formula 1

Troubleshooter

✂

A kitten is stuck at the top of a tree in the next door neighbour's garden.

Mum has accidentally locked the car keys inside the car.

A floppy disk is stuck in the disk drive of your computer.

You made 10 sausage rolls and 15 people have turned up for the picnic.

The cat has trodden on the birthday card you made for Nan.

The new sofa has arrived, but it won't fit through the front door.

Gran phones to say she has locked herself out of her house.

A tree has blown down in the garden, blocking the gateway.

You arrive back from holiday with someone else's suitcase.

You promised to make a cake for the school fair, but there's a power cut.

You left the box of crackers in the garage and the rain
leaked in during the night, soaking the box.

Auntie Jane took her nephews two packets of sweets,
but when she got there, they had a friend round to play.

Nan knitted a cardigan for the baby, but it's far too small.

You get exactly the same present from two different people.

Speechmark Ⓢ Ⓟ This page may be photocopied for instructional use only.

PAGE 257

Understanding & Using Spoken Language © C Delamain & J Spring 2004

Stage IV

Reporting
& Debating

Persuaders

Chocolate ice-cream is the best.

Playstations are better than television.

There is definitely life on Mars.

Aliens have visited the Earth.

Dogs make better pets than cats.

Football is the best sport.

'Blue Peter' is a cool programme.

Baby sisters are more fun than baby brothers.

Dinosaurs never existed.

The Loch Ness Monster is real.

You won't get a cold if you stay indoors.

Doing a paper round is a great job.

Gel pens are better than felt-tips.

Adidas® trainers are the best.

The best way to travel is by train.

You can't make a fire without matches.

It's possible to grow cress in the dark.

All gardens should have a climbing frame.

Banana milkshakes are best.

Gardens should be free of all insects.

Point of View

Stage IV

Reporting & Debating

FARMER SEES ENORMOUS BEAST NEAR SHEEP

farmer

animal conservationist

HEAD TEACHER AGREES TO NO UNIFORM

pupil on school council

teacher

SUPERMARKET GIVES KIDS FREE CHOCOLATE

dentist

child

SKATEBOARDS ALLOWED ON PAVEMENTS

teenager

old lady

TEENAGER JUMPS ON CAR ROOF

teenager's mother

the police

SCHOOL WILL CLOSE AT 2.00 PM

parent

child

TEACHERS BAN TELEVISION AT HOME

parent

head teacher

Stage I

Using
Speech
Effectively

Volume Control (1)

1 As the children went into the cave, they could hear a distant booming – **boom, boom, boom**. The goblins were hammering. The children's feet rang on the stones – **clang, clang** – and they were afraid the goblins would hear them. As they got nearer, the **whooshing** sound of the waterfall grew louder and louder.

2 Jack knocked very loudly on the door – **ratatat, ratatat!** Nobody answered. He rang the bell – **brrr, brrr**. Still no reply. Reaching up to the window, Jack banged on it as hard as he could – **bang, bang, bang**. At this, an upstairs window opened and a voice shouted, '**Go away boy, or you'll be sorry**!'

3 Grandma was dozing on the sofa. She was snoring pretty loudly. (**zzzzzzzzzzzzz**) 'Wake up, Grandma', said Chloe. 'It's time for tea.' Grandma's eyes stayed shut. '**Wake up, Grandma**', said Chloe, more loudly. Grandma went on snoring. '**Grandma, wake up!**' shouted Chloe, '**It's time for tea!**' Grandma woke with a jump. '**There's no need to shout**', she yelled, '**Do you think I'm deaf or something**?'

4 The firework display was great. One after another the rockets went off – **whizz** – **bang** – **flash** – and the children went '**ooh**!' with excitement. The bonfire burned brighter and brighter, until the last logs fell in and there was a last mighty **crackling** sound. Then the last golden rain went **whee,** and there was an '**aah!**' from the crowd**.** The firework man banged a gong for silence – **bang, bong**. Then he shouted '**That's it, everyone! Time to go home!**'

Volume Control (1) *(continued)*

Stage I

Using
Speech
Effectively

✂- -

5 Auntie Jo's baby was asleep at last. *'Sshh'* ,said Mum softly. *'For goodness sake don't wake him up.'* At that moment the postman banged on the door. Susie *tiptoed* to answer it. She opened it as quietly as she could, but it still gave its usual little *squeak*. *'Please don't wake the baby'*, she said in her smallest voice, *'He's been awake all night.'*

6 The children were playing hide-and-seek, but Harry hadn't really got the idea. He had been told he had to call 'Cuckoo', but he did it so quietly nobody could hear him. *'Cuckoo, cuckoo'*, went this tiny little voice. Then, getting worried because nobody came *'Cooee! Cooee!'* The others were searching in all the wrong places. *'I'm in this cupboard'*, said the little voice, *'And I want to be found*!'

7 *'I'm sure we've got mice'*, said Dad over breakfast. *'You just listen tonight'*. Jake lay in bed that night, listening as hard as he could. Sure enough, there came a *pitter-patter* of mousey feet above his head. Then he heard a soft *scritch-scratch*, and a sort of *scuffle-scuffle*. Jake got out of bed and *crept* silently to the door of his bedroom. He switched on the light with a little *click*. The sounds from the attic stopped.

8 Kemal had never been in a boat this big before. The engine was switched off, and the boat was slipping along under sail. From inside the cabin, all he could hear was the gentle *slap-slap* of the waves, the *mew-mew* of the seagulls, and the soft *pad-pad* of Rashid's bare feet on the deck. Ahmed was asleep on the other bunk. Then Kemal heard Rashid calling quietly to him: *'Come up on deck. I want to show you something.'* Up on deck, Kemal looked where Rashid was pointing. *'Keep quiet'*, Rashid whispered, *'and watch.'*

Stage I

Using
Speech
Effectively

Moody (1)

1 It was a sad, sad day when Arthur's gerbil died. That morning the rain poured down steadily, the sky was dark grey, and Arthur's heart was as heavy as lead. He buried poor old Whiffles in the garden, under an apple tree, and placed a stone over him, saying: 'Here lies Whiffles. A long-lost friend.'

2 The night was very dark. The wind moaned in the chimney. The doors creaked, and the inn sign groaned to and fro. In the corner, the old man sat sighing over his beer. He had lost all his money. 'Ten pounds gone, all my spare money for this week, all gone on the lottery.' He heaved another sigh, and a tear trickled slowly down his cheeks.

3 Emily waved and waved as the big boat sailed slowly out of the harbour. Soon she could hardly see her friend standing by the railings. Emily felt like crying. She knew she would not see Tia again for a long, long time; maybe never. She had been her best friend, and now Emily felt very much alone.

4 Jake had eaten much too much cake. Then he had eaten too many chocolates, and now he felt as if he had swallowed a huge big lump of concrete. He lay down on the sofa and closed his eyes. His tummy ached dreadfully, his head ached, and he felt sick. 'Why was I such an idiot', he groaned.

Moody (1) *(continued)*

Stage I

Using
Speech
Effectively

✂- -

5 The old house was coming down. This was the house where Jamie had been born, and he had always lived here. Now it was being knocked down to make way for a new road. With every bit that fell, Jamie felt a memory being ground into nothing. Tears filled his eyes as he saw his bedroom wall, with the aeroplane wallpaper that he loved, crumbling into dust.

6 All day the little bird had been busy fetching worms for her babies. Now one little featherless baby had fallen out of the nest, and was dead on the stones. By the end of the day, two more had fallen out, and the poor little mother bird had only one left. Still she went on, bravely fetching worms for her last little fledgling.

Stage I

Using
Speech
Effectively

Double Spinner

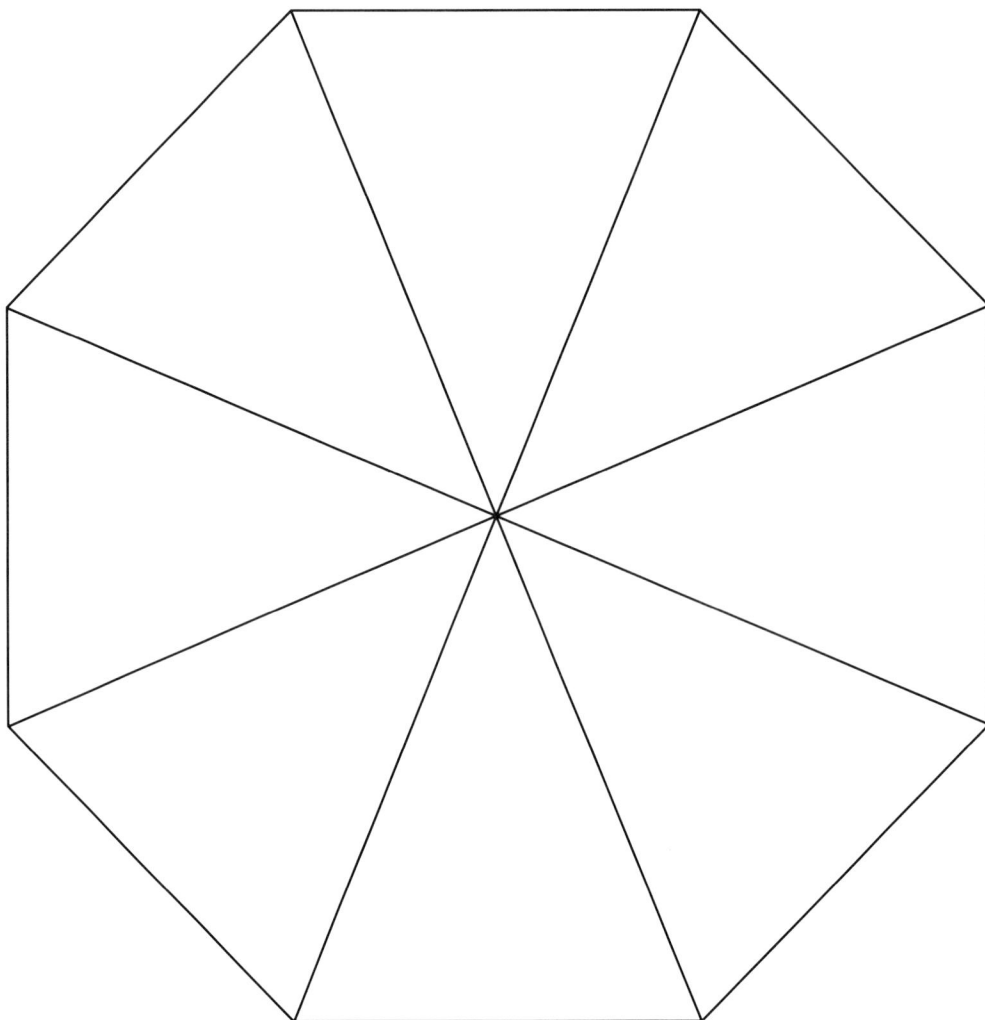

Whisperer

Stage I

Using Speech Effectively

Bounce the ball.	Throw the bean-bag to the teacher.
Balance the bean-bag on your head.	Throw the ball into the air and catch it again.
Roll the ball across the floor.	Balance the bean-bag on your left shoulder.
Bounce the ball three times.	Throw the bean-bag into the air and catch it again.
Throw the bean-bag to the teacher.	Roll the ball to the back of the line.
Put the bean-bag on your right foot.	Kick the ball forwards.
Kick the ball sideways.	Pick up the bean-bag, and drop it on the floor.
Throw the bean-bag to someone in the line.	Kick the ball backwards.
Drop the ball on to the bean-bag.	Carry the ball to the teacher.
Balance the bean-bag on your knee.	Put the ball and the bean-bag in front of the teacher.

Stage I

Using
Speech
Effectively

Express Train

This activity is really choral speaking. To give the children the idea of speeding up or slowing down their speech, try this: tell them that an engine is going up a steep hill, getting slower and slower as it pulls its load to the top. As it goes, it repeats to itself, 'I think I can do it, I think I can do it, I think I can do it', more and more slowly, until it is almost at a standstill. As it reaches the top, it changes its little chant to, 'I thought I could, I thought I could, I thought I could', saying it faster and faster as it gathers speed down the other side of the hill. Get the children to practise this, perhaps all together at first, then with one group saying, 'I think I can do it', and another group saying, 'I thought I could'.

You can use the 'train noises' in any way you choose – you might decide to have several groups all saying different sounds, getting faster and faster; some starting fast and slowing down; some starting a few seconds after another group – its up to you!

Trickety-track Clickety-clack Trackety-trick
Clackety-click Tootety-toot   Rattety-tat

Volume Control (2)

Stage II

Using
Speech
Effectively

Front: A magic ice-cream van has just pulled up outside the
           school. If anyone would like an ice-cream, say 'Yes!' now.

Middle: We might go to a theme park, or to the seaside this term.
           If you would like to go to a theme park, put up your hand.

Back: If you think you have deserved an extra-long playtime
           tomorrow, stand up now.

Front: Any minute now, a scary monster will fly in at the window
           and out at the other side of the classroom (or hall). If you
           don't want to see it, shut your eyes.

Middle: If you know your whole address and post-code, put both
           hands on top of your head.

Back: If you are seven or eight years old, stand up, and put one
           hand in the air.

Stage II

Using
Speech
Effectively

Moody (2)

1 Pippa was so excited about her birthday party. The room where the tea was laid out was prettily decorated, with pink and purple balloons and paper streamers. Cakes, sandwiches and jellies were all ready. Peeping out of the window, Pippa thought she saw the first people arriving. Her mum was still in her bedroom, putting on her party clothes. Pippa ran to the bottom of the stairs and called up, 'Mum! Quick! Hurry up! People are coming!'

2 It was the day of the big parade. Tim was up on the balcony, looking down on a street full of streamers, balloons and ticker-tape. He could just hear the pipes and drums of the band coming round the corner, and the crowd beginning to cheer. Soon everyone was waving their flags and jumping up and down. Now Tim saw the first float, the one his Dad was on. It looked amazing, and Tim clapped and clapped, until his hands were sore.

3 It was the school Sports Day. Poppy's little brother, Pete, was going to run in the sack race. Mrs Brown's flag went down, her whistle blew, and they were off! Pete kept going faster and faster, as, one after another, the children tripped and fell over. Now he was out in front! Poppy was screaming in her excitement, 'Come on Pete!' Keep going! You're going to win!'

4 Lucy was learning to ice-skate. She was getting better and better, and one day her teacher decided to set a little dance to music for her. After a little practice, Lucy began to swoop and turn and glide in time with the music. Faster went the music, faster went Lucy's skates, until she felt as if she was flying. As the last bars of the music played, Lucy whizzed across the rink like a bird – too fast to stop! She grabbed at the crash barrier, and came down with a bump.

Speechmark (P)

Moody (2) *(continued)*

5 Callum's Dad had taken him to a race meeting. Callum had put a 10p bet with his Dad that the jockey with the black and red colours would win. The horses were coming up the last slope. Callum's horse was lying third. As Callum watched, the jockey shook the reins, and the horse surged forward. Past the second horse, past the first one – Callum's horse was in front by a whisker as he swept past the finishing post.

6 The jumbo jet's engines were running. Nathan heard the pilot talking to the cabin crew. 'Prepare for take off', he said. In the cabin the message came on: 'Fasten your seat belts'. The plane began to roll down the runway, gathering speed until the runway lights were flashing past too quickly to count. The plane's nose lifted, they were going up and up, and peering out of the window, Nathan saw ships as tiny as toys out on the sea.

7 The curtains opened and the clowns came tumbling in, leaping, turning somersaults, and falling over their feet. The smallest one, Bobo, set off round the ring at top speed, chased by another one carrying a bucket of water. All of a sudden, Bobo tripped and fell, and with a mighty splash the bucket of water was tipped all over him. With a yell, Bobo was up and after his attacker, who turned and fled with his trousers falling down.

8 Peter Pan was in real trouble. He was up against the rigging of the pirate ship, he'd dropped his sword, and Hook was coming at him with a grin of triumph on his face. Then they heard it – tick, tock, tick, tock. 'The crocodile's coming, the crocodile's coming', shouted the children. 'Look behind you!' Hook swung round, and turned pale as the crocodile waddled closer.

Beat out the Rhythm

Stage II

Using
Speech
Effectively

There **was** a young **la**dy from **Ryde**,

Who ate **for**ty green **app**les and **died**.

The **app**les fer**men**ted

In**side** the la**men**ted,

And made **ci**der in**side** her in**side**.

There **once** was a **fel**low from **Twick**enham,

Whose **boots** were too **tight** to walk **quick** in 'em.

He **went** for a **mile**,

And sat **down** on a **stile**

And **took** off his **boots** and was **sick** in 'em.

There **was** an old **per**son of **Fra**tton,

Who **would** go to **church** with his **hat** on.

'If I **wake** up', he **said**

'With my **hat** on my **head**,

I'll **know** that it **has**n't been **sat** on.'

There **was** a young **la**dy from **Ri**ga,

Who **went** for a **ride** on a **ti**ger.

By the **end** of the **ride**,

The **girl** is in**side** –

There's a **smile** on the **face** of the **ti**ger.

Speechmark   **P** This page may be photocopied for instructional use only.
Understanding & Using Spoken Language © C Delamain & J Spring 2004

Beat out the Rhythm *(continued)*

Stage II

Using
Speech
Effectively

✂ -

A **lus**ty young **fe**llow from **Slough**,

At**tem**pted to **ride** on a **cow**.

The **poor** chap fell **off**,

In the **cow's** water **trough**.

He **said**, 'I'll just **have** to learn **how'**.

- -

The **was** a young **man** who said, '**Drat**!

I'm **get**ting so **ter**ribly **fat**.

I'll **keep** these baked-**beans**,

And a **hand**ful of gree**n**s,

And I'll **just** have to **live** upon **that'**.

- -

A **care**less young **boy** shouted, '**Drat**!

I've **squashed** your poor **ham**ster quite **flat'**.

Said **Mum**, 'What a **shame**,

But **you** aren't to **blame**,

And I **ra**ther pre**fer** him like **that'**.

Stage II

Using
Speech
Effectively

Messengers (1)

Get your coat, it's time to go.	Come and sit down, tea is ready.
Can you help me find the car key?	Look, it's snowing!
Would you like a chocolate?	Let's go out in the garden.
It's really cold, you need a coat.	The road ahead is flooded.
I need to speak to you.	Who put that on the table?
Don't forget to shut the door.	We will need notebooks and pens.
How long until we get there?	Be careful, it's breakable.
If you've finished, you can go out.	I think we've got a flat tyre.
Grandad, who is deaf	The head teacher
A three-year-old child	Your best friend

Goatherds

Stage II

Using Speech Effectively

Goats' Names:

Bumble, Grumble, Mumble, Bubble

Squeaky, Creaky, Seeky, Sleeky

Potty, Poppy, Stroppy, Soppy

Grinny, Brinny, Prinny, Drinny

Beadle, Beagle, Beetle, Beale

Happy, Hatty, Hassy, Haffy

Ikey, Pikey, Tikey, Likey

Understanding & Using Spoken Language © C Delamain & J Spring 2004

Ring the Changes

Where have I put my blue jumper this time?

Where have I put my blue jumper this time?
Where have I put my blue jumper **this** time?
Where **have** I put my blue jumper this time?
Where have I put my **blue** jumper this time?
Where have **I** put my blue jumper this time?
Where have I put my blue **jumper** this time?

Why can't we go to the cinema next Thursday?

Why can't we go to the cinema next Thursday?
Why **can't** we go to the cinema next Thursday?
Why can't **we** go to the cinema next Thursday?
Why can't we go to the **cinema** next Thursday?
Why can't we go to the cinema **next** Thursday?
Why can't we go to the cinema next **Thursday**?

What do you think you're doing playing about up there at midnight?

What do you think you're doing, playing about up there at midnight?
What **do** you think you're doing, playing about up there at midnight?
What do **you** think you're doing, playing about up there at midnight?
What do you think you're **doing,** playing about up there at midnight?
What do you think you're doing, playing about up **there** at midnight?
What do you think you're doing, playing about up there at **midnight**?

When do you think Grandma could possibly arrive?

When do you think Grandma could possibly arrive?
When **do** you think Grandma could possibly arrive?
When do you **think** Grandma could possibly arrive?
When do you think **Grandma** could possibly arrive?
When do you think Grandma could **possibly** arrive?
When do you think Grandma could possibly **arrive**?

Speechmark Ⓟ

Correct Me!

Stage III

Using
Speech
Effectively

My nan broke her leg and she is in *hostable*.	There is an absolutely *normous* spider in the bath.
At the zoo we saw monkeys, *efelants* and giraffes.	My mum always cooks *biscetti* on Saturdays.
Mary and *Jovis* went to Bethlehem on a donkey.	An eight-sided shape is called an *oxagon*.
We've got a new *'pooter* in our classroom.	Draw a *diabonal* line across the page.
The Queen lives in *Bunkingham* Palace.	Put your football shirt in the washing *'chine*.
We are going to make *pamcakes* for tea.	In Science we learnt about *epavoration*.
Air *ristance* makes a parachute stay up in the air.	I like cereal and toast for *bekfast*.
The *gerontosaurus* was a plant-eating dinosaur.	*Transfarent* means you can see through something.
I am going to play on my *scapeboard* tonight.	A round 3D shape is called a *sophia*.
Information books are called *non-friction*.	*Janry* is the first month of the year.
Cola bears live in Australia.	The Atlantic and the *Specific* are big oceans.
Mount Everest is in the *Hilamayas*.	Little Miss *Muppet* sat on a tuffet.
Doctors use a *sethoscope* to listen to your heart.	A violin is a musical *instament*.
A *majfying* glass makes things bigger.	My cousin is a *vegenarian*.
Use a *tescolope* to look at the stars.	I got a *ditigal* camera for Christmas.
We made electrical *critics* in Science.	We saw a *hittopotamus* at the zoo.

Stage III

Using
Speech
Effectively

Wordpix

Examples

L △ec △tris △it E

el   ec   tric   it   y

K   **9**

ca   nine

A ◯ in A 🐂

a   bom   in   a   ble

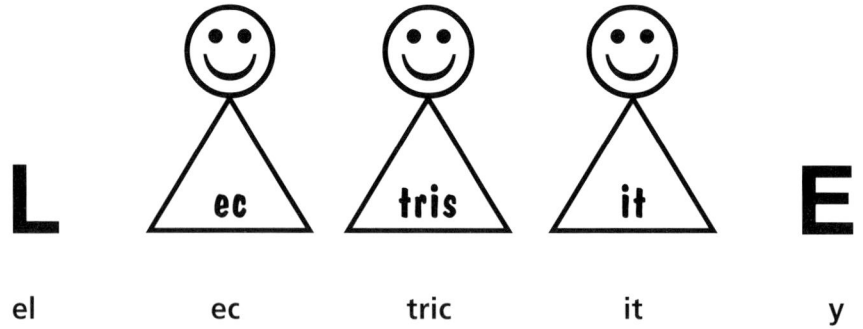

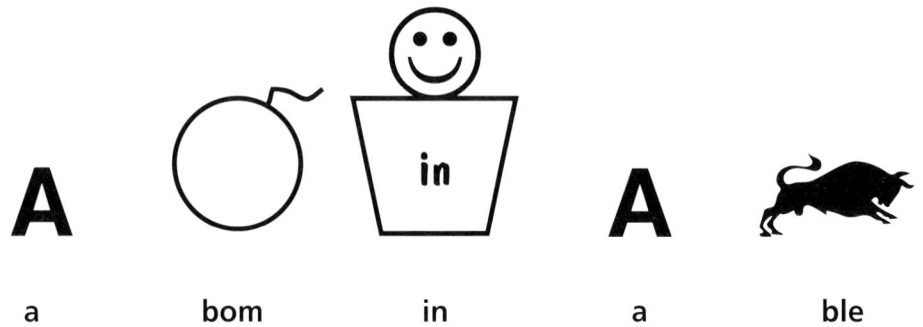

NB These are just a few ideas to start you off. Any visual representation of a syllable or syllables will work.

Wordpix *(continued)*

Stage III

Using
Speech
Effectively

Sample Word List

electricity	estimate
condensation	horizontal
evaporation	vertical
reversible	diagonal
irreversible	calculator
circulation	circumference
oxygen	diameter
germination	experiment
pollination	investigation
gravity	quadrilateral
resistance	hexagonal
attraction	triangular
repulsion	approximately
aluminium	environmental
flexibility	tributary
polystyrene	conservation
thermometer	reservoir
temperature	population
canine	architecture
rotation	evacuee
sphere	agriculture
spherical	invention

PAGE 277

Stage III

Using
Speech
Effectively

Tangled Tongues

Sister Susie's sewing socks for sailors. Where are the sailors' socks Sister Susie sewed?

Which switch is the switch Miss for Ipswich? It's the Ipswich switch which I require.

What noise annoys an oyster most? A noisy noise annoys an oyster most.

How much wood could a woodchuck chuck, it a woodchuck could chuck wood?

She sells sea shells on the sea shore, and the shells she sells are seashells I'm sure.

Whose wrist watch is a Swiss wrist watch, and are you sure it's a Swiss wrist watch?

Theophilus Thistle was a thistle sifter, and he sifted thirty thousand thistles thoroughly.

Millions of mixed biscuits, mixed up in a mixed biscuit box.

Peter Piper picked a peck of pickled peppers, so where's the peck of pickled peppers Peter Piper picked?

The soldier had a sore shoulder, and the soldier's shoulder was surely sore.

Six sick sea serpents slithered into the shiny sea.

Done to a T

Stage III

Using Speech Effectively

Pitter –	– patter
Helter –	– skelter
Water –	– beetle
Nitty –	– gritty
Hoity –	– toity
Arty –	– tarty
Flitter –	– flutter
Water –	– buttercup
Water –	– meter
Water –	– heater
Letter –	– writer

You can continue this using two part words in which only one part contains a medial 't' – for example, 'egg-beater', 'party-pooper', 'litter-basket'.

Make a Play

1 Tom and Jaz were bored. They wanted something exciting to happen. Jaz thought they should go to the park, but Tom said they weren't allowed to. There was a knock at the door. Jaz opened it. Mrs Smith and her daughter, Lu, stood on the doorstep. Mrs Smith looked really excited. She nudged Lu and told her to tell them the news. Lu told them they had won a trip to Eurodisney, for four people. Just then a car stopped. Tom and Jaz recognised the sound of mum's car. She had just come back from a shopping trip with Gran. As they got out of the car, Gran announced that she couldn't find her glasses. Mum asked her when she last had them.

2 It was the first day of the summer holidays. Lee and Josh were getting ready to go fishing. Lee wondered if they should take an umbrella. Josh was more worried about how many sandwiches they would need. When they got to the river, there were two men already sitting on the bank. One was dozing, the other staring at the river. When he felt a tug on his line he nudged his friend excitedly. They discussed how big the fish would be as they wound in the line. Suddenly there was a shout from further up the river bank. A couple of teenage boys had been throwing stones and one of them had slipped. He yelled to his friend that he couldn't swim. His friend knew he needed to get help.

3 Mr and Mrs Jones were busy in their garden. It was a sunny day, but then a big black cloud appeared. Mrs Jones wondered if she should get the washing in before it rained. Mr Jones wanted to get the grass cut. Next door the Singh twins were having a water fight. Maya was angry because Ravi had squirted water all over her Barbie® doll. Ravi said it was her own fault for leaving it on the grass. Mr Singh leant out of the upstairs window and complained about the water all over the patio. At that moment there was a flash of lightning and heavy drops of rain started to fall. Mrs Singh called the children in for tea.

4 It was playtime. Gemma and Nita wanted someone to turn the long rope, so that they could play a skipping game. They went round the playground asking for volunteers. In the end Zeb and Ram, two boys in the year above, agreed to turn the rope. It started off well, then Zeb had an idea. He told Ram. Ram said he would count to three. The two girls both tripped over the speeding rope. One of the assistants came to see if the girls were hurt. Another assistant managed to catch the boys, just as they were trying to sneak away.

Choose Your Words!

I mean	
Sort of	
You know	
Like	
Well	
Stuff	

Stage IV

Using
Speech
Effectively

Messengers (2)

Messages

Please shut the window, it's cold.

What time is the next bus?

Move over, I'm squashed.

Have you see my book anywhere?

There isn't any milk left.

Tell me your email address.

How long until we get there?

I thought the film was a bit boring.

What kind of music do you like?

Be careful, the path is slippery.

This phone isn't working properly.

I haven't got time to do it now.

a French exchange pupil	a school inspector
a five-year-old boy	a supply teacher

Story Crowd

Characters

Gollum	Cruella de Vil
Captain Hook	Bart Simpson
The Giant (Jack and the Beanstalk)	Donald Duck
Barbie®	Baby Bear (Goldilocks)

Messages

Who would like an ice-cream?

Can you tell me the way to the shops?

The music is too loud.

I don't like tomato sandwiches.

My phone needs charging.

The car won't start.

Is it too late to see the film?

Where is my umbrella?

UNDERSTANDING SPOKEN LANGUAGE: RECORD SHEET

Key: needs adult support ◰ almost achieved ⊠ achieved ▩

Child's Name	Active Listening & Memory				Thinking & Reasoning				Word Play			
	I	II	III	IV	I	II	III	IV	I	II	III	IV

USING SPOKEN LANGUAGE: RECORD SHEET

Key: needs adult support ◹ almost achieved ⊠ achieved ■

Child's Name	Explaining & Describing				Reporting & Debating				Using Speech Effectively			
	I	II	III	IV	I	II	III	IV	I	II	III	IV

Bibliography

Ackroyd J, 2000, *Literacy Alive!,* Hodder and Stoughton, London.

Berger A & Gross G, 1999, *Teaching the Literacy Hour in an Inclusive Classroom,* David Fulton Publications, London.

Booth D, *Reading the Stories we Construct Together,* Hodder and Stoughton, London.

Crystal D, 1987, *The Cambridge Encyclopaedia of Language*, Cambridge University Press, Cambridge.

Delamain C & Spring J, 2000, *Developing Baseline Communication Skills,* Speechmark Publishing Ltd, Bicester.

Delamain C & Spring J, 2003, *Games for Speaking, Listening and Understanding*, Speechmark Publishing Ltd, Bicester.

DfES, 2003, *Speaking, Listening, Learning; Working with Children in Key Stage 1 & 2*, Qualifications and Curriculum Authority, London.

Fleming P, Miller C & Wright J, 1997, *Speech and Language Difficulties in Education*, Winslow Press, Chesterfield.

Johnson M, 1991,1992, *Functional Language in the Classroom*, Manchester Metropolitan University Publishers.

Lock A, Ginsborg J & Peers I, 2002, 'Development and Disadvantage: Implications for the Early Years and Beyond', *International Journal of Language and Communication Disorders*, 37(1).

Martin D, 2000, *Teaching Children with Speech and Language Difficulties*, David Fulton Publishers, London.

Martin D & Miller C, 2002, *Speech and Language Difficulties in the Classroom,* David Fulton Publishers, London.

McMinn J, 2002, *Supporting Children with Speech and Language Disorders and Associated,* David Fulton Publishers, London.

Pinker S, 1999, *Words and Rules,* Weidenfeld & Nicholson, London.

Sage R, 2000, *The Communication Opportunity Group Scheme*, Leicester University Press, Leicester.

Stackhouse J & Wells B, 1997, *Children's Speech and Literacy Difficulties Book 2 – Identification and Intervention,* Whurr Publications, London.

Stuart L, Wright P, Grigor S & Howey A, 2002, *Spoken Language Difficulties*, David Fulton Publishers, London.

Wright J & Kersner M, 1988, *Supporting Children with Communication Problems,* David Fulton Publishers, London.

Using & Understanding Language

Speaking, Listening & Understanding

Games for Young Children (5 to 7 Year Olds)

Catherine Delamain & Jill Spring

Linked to the school curriculum, this book is easy to follow and will supply you with fun games to develop receptive and expressive language and skills. This is a resource that can be used in structured planning of classroom activities as well as on the spur of the moment.

It has a structured progression as well as information on assessment, target setting and evaluation.

Ideal for 5 to 7 year olds, the activities can be adapted for use with older children with language delay. Photocopiable support sheets are provided, and each activity has a clear aim, simple instructions and requires minimal equipment.

"The children enjoyed the games we were able to play and are looking forward to trying more!"

– Hobby Horse Children's Centre

Winner of the 2004 Education Resources: Primary Books Award

WINNER 2004

Highly Commended in the Books for Learning & Teaching category of the 2004 TES/NASEN Special Needs Book Awards

Understanding & Using Spoken Language

New for 2004

Games for 7 to 9 Year Olds

Catherine Delamain & Jill Spring

Following on from *Speaking, Listening & Understanding*, this book has games for older children (7–9 year olds) and again links with the school curriculum.

These games will improve children's understanding and use of spoken language and provide you with ready-to-use classroom activities that enable you to focus on speaking and listening skills. Ideal for setting targets, each skill area is organised along broad developmental lines and the activities are designed to be incorporated into the daily classroom programme.

Instructions are clear and simple, the equipment needed is kept to a minimum and the majority of the resources are provided as photocopiable pages.

Developing Baseline Communication Skills

Catherine Delamain & Jill Spring

This practical resource will foster personal and social development and improve the language and early literacy skills of children aged 4–5. You can also adapt the activities for use with older children with language delay or communication difficulties.

Containing two hundred games that are graded into levels of difficulty, this resource will give you quick and easy activities that can be easily incorporated into the school curriculum. Each activity clearly states the area of focus, the difficulty level and where it will fit with the curriculum (whether circle time, literacy hour, outdoor play, hall and PE, topic work, drama or small group work). In the Personal and Social Development section activities cover turn taking, body language, awareness of others, confidence and independence, feelings and emotions, and in Language and Literacy, the games will develop understanding, listening and attention, speaking, auditory memory and phonological awareness.

Recognising your time-constraints, equipment is not needed or kept to a minimum, record keeping is simple and minimal, and the games can be mostly organised by classroom assistants or volunteers.

Speechmark